STECK-VAUGHN

LANGUAGE
ARTS
SOLUTIONS

Go Grammar!

Green Level

Rigby • Saxon • Steck-Vaughn

www.HarcourtAchieve.com
1.800.531.5015

Go Grammar! Green Level
Steck-Vaughn Language Arts Solutions

© 2002 Thomson Learning Australia
Exclusive United States Distribution: Harcourt Achieve Inc.

© 2006 Harcourt Achieve Inc.

1 2 3 4 5 6 7 8 9 10 054 10 09 08 07 06 05

Printed in the United States of America

ISBN 1-4190-1246-0

Contents

Common Nouns

A **common noun** is any word that names a person, place, creature, thing, feeling, idea, or quality.

Example   The **children** watch the **movements** of the **gorillas** at the **zoo**.

Capitalize a common noun when it starts a sentence.

Example   **Students** enter a world of the imagination when they read alone.

Try It Out

1   The word search below contains nine common nouns that would be found in a cookbook. Circle the words. Then, write them in a list below.

A	S	P	A	R	A	G	U	S
L	Q	O	P	U	H	C	L	B
M	E	O	P	E	P	P	E	R
O	M	I	L	K	W	M	M	E
N	L	F	E	G	G	L	O	A
D	F	L	O	U	R	A	N	D

_____

_____

2   Now use at least four nouns from the word search to write a sentence about your favorite meal, real or imaginary.

_____

_____

Taking It Further

There is a simple way to identify a noun. If you can put *the*, *a*, or *an* before a word, that word is a noun.

Example   I like eating **a** banana in **the** morning. (*A* and *the* go before *banana* and *morning;* therefore, these words are nouns.)

If a word can be made into a plural (more than one) by adding an *s*, then that word is a noun.

Example   I like eating **bananas** in the morning. (*Banana* can be made plural by adding *s;* therefore, *banana* is a noun.)

Find and circle twenty common nouns in the following news report. The names of people and places are proper nouns (see Lesson 2) and should not be circled.

Students from Arbor Middle School soaked up some local color and left some behind when they visited Botanica Lake recently. The group joined Friends of Botanica Lake to plant trees and remove trash during the first weekend of fall. Their teacher, Ms. Pinewood, said the visit provided a great opportunity for the class to give back to nature.

"The students love to get outside the classroom and many of them learned how to plant a young sapling and enjoy the outdoors. Some of them are also writing a musical called *Botanica Lake Fantasy* about the place, its plants, and its wildlife," Ms. Pinewood said.

In the Real World

Imagine you want to describe the front of your house or apartment building for a friend or relative who is coming to visit. Write your description on the lines provided. Use 40 words or fewer, and include at least five common nouns in your description.

Example   My **house** is **part** of a **duplex**. The **front** is covered with **wood** and **stone**, and the **trim** is dark green.

_____

_____

_____

_____

LESSON 2 # Proper Nouns
NOUNS AND PRONOUNS

> **Proper nouns** name a particular person, place, thing, business, or organization.
>
> **Example**   Some **Olympians,** like **Ian Thorpe,** become media celebrities while pursuing their athletic goals.
>
> They also name days and months (but not seasons).
>
> **Example**   Many people hope for snow in the winter months of **December** and **January**.
>
> Proper nouns always start with a capital letter, either in a sentence or standing alone.
>
> **Example**   Before probes photographed its surface, **Mars** was truly an alien world.

Try It Out

Write down the correct proper noun in each column below. Check an atlas to match each country and capital city correctly.

Country	Capital City
Canada	
Mexico	
	San Salvador
	Quito
Jamaica	
Cuba	
	Port-au-Prince
Argentina	
Chile	
	Lima

Taking It Further

The following student's e-mail message does not bother with capitalizing proper nouns and words at the beginning of sentences. Rewrite it with correct capitalization on the lines provided.

hey, sylvia,

today in class, we talked about the end of the first world war. the league of nations was formed to promote peace and cooperation, but it didn't last. although president woodrow wilson helped found it, the united states was never a member of it. the united nations replaced it.

hope that helps,

monika

_____

_____

_____

_____

_____

_____

In the Real World

Choose a city that you would like to visit. Find out about two attractions in the city. Then, on the lines provided, write a brief description that includes at least three proper nouns. Locate an interesting visual to go with your description.

Example   I'd love to visit **San Francisco,** particularly two special places: **Golden Gate Park,** which includes a beautiful Japanese tea garden, and **Alcatraz,** the famous prison that held criminals like **Al Capone.**

_____

_____

_____

_____

NAME _____   DATE _____

LESSON 3 — Concrete and Abstract Nouns
NOUNS AND PRONOUNS

> A **concrete noun** names something that can be seen, heard, tasted, felt, or smelled.
>
> **Examples**   desk   friend   overpass   flame
>
> An **abstract noun** names something that cannot be perceived by one of the senses. An abstract noun often names a feeling, idea, or quality. Notice that when used in this way, abstract nouns cannot be counted or made plural.
>
> **Examples**   joy   doubt   freedom   compassion

Try It Out

1   Below are five abstract nouns and five concrete nouns taken from a discussion of television viewing. Write each noun in the correct column below.

station   familiarity   camera   mood   sympathy

humor   music   make-up   lights   awareness

Abstract Nouns	Concrete Nouns

2   Choose a character from a book, television show, or movie. Use abstract nouns to name three of the character's strengths and three weaknesses, and write them in the appropriate columns below.

Title: _____

Character: _____

Strengths	Weaknesses

Taking It Further

1   Circle the abstract nouns in the passage below.

> Are cell phones about convenience or annoyance? Many schools have banned
> mobile phones because of the distraction they can cause. However, safety is
> also an important concern. Some parents want their children to have a quick
> means of communication in case of an emergency.

2   Write one or two sentences about your view on cell phone use.

_____

_____

_____

In the Real World

Either on your own or in small groups, explore the issue of cell phones. Then, plan a brief
argument either for or against allowing cell phones in school. Express your view in the form
of a letter to the editor of a newspaper. Your letter should try to persuade readers to agree
with you. Include at least three abstract nouns.

Dear Editor:

_____

_____

_____

_____

_____

_____

_____

_____

_____

LESSON 4 **NOUNS AND PRONOUNS**

Collective Nouns

Collective nouns name groups of people, animals, or objects. A singular verb follows a collective noun if it refers to the group as a whole. A plural verb follows a collective noun if it refers to the individual members or parts of the group.

Example A **litter** of newborn puppies **was** nestled in the basket.
The **audience have** finally taken their seats.

Try It Out

The word search below contains seven collective nouns. Circle the words. Then, below the word search, fill in each blank with the correct collective noun for the animals or people indicated. You may use a dictionary to find definitions of the collective nouns.

C	P	R	I	D	E
O	A	M	C	A	F
L	C	O	A	P	L
O	K	J	S	G	O
N	E	S	T	O	C
Y	H	E	R	D	K

1 _____ of ants/penguins

2 _____ of cattle

3 _____ of sheep

4 _____ of wolves

5 _____ of lions

6 _____ of actors/players

7 _____ of mice/wasps

Taking It Further

The writer of the following dream poem has seriously confused some collective nouns. Circle the incorrect collective nouns, and rewrite the poem so that it makes sense. Use a dictionary or the Internet to check the collective nouns.

Shipwrecked on a tropical island,
serenaded by a pod of gulls on the wing
and a flock of dolphins at sea,
sure that a fleet of cards
was my only other companion,
I was amazed to spy a deck of ships
sailing on the horizon!

_____

_____

_____

_____

_____

_____

In the Real World

Find out to which group of people the following collective nouns refer. Then, write your answers in the columns below. You may use a dictionary to help you.

Collective noun	Group of people	Collective noun	Group of people
board		cortege	
crew		faculty	
troupe		class	
panel		congregation	

LESSON 5 # Personal Pronouns
NOUNS AND PRONOUNS

> **Pronouns** are used in place of nouns. **Personal pronouns** stand for nouns that name people, animals, or things.
>
> **Example**   **They** told **me** I can improve **it**.
>
> Personal pronouns are usually labeled according to
> - **person** (first person is the person speaking, second person is the person being spoken to, and the third person is the person or thing being spoken about)
> - **gender** (masculine, feminine, or neuter)
> - **number** (singular or plural).
>
> | | Singular | | Plural | |
> |---|---|---|---|---|
> | | **Subject** | **Object** | **Subject** | **Object** |
> | **1st person** | I | me | we | us |
> | **2nd person** | you | you | you | you |
> | **3rd person** | he/she/it | him/her/it | they | them |

Try It Out

1   Write the correct form of the personal pronoun in each sentence.

a The students have studied hard, but will _____ score higher on this test?

b My dad gave me two gift certificates, and I gave one of _____ to my sister for her birthday.

c As treasurer, I'm annoyed that some club members have not yet paid _____ their yearly fees.

d If _____ can't stand the heat, get out of the kitchen!

e Please drop _____ in the box on your way out or show me tomorrow.

f Our teacher told _____ to straighten our backs when using the computer.

2 Circle the personal pronouns in the following newspaper report.

Regarding the proposed highway, Mr. Johnson said, "We don't see any problem with it. Local businesses and homeowners say they can tolerate the inconvenience. In the long run, the road will help all of us get around the city, you included."

Taking It Further

Interview a student in your class or a member of your family and write his or her reply to this question: What do you enjoy most about your hobby, sport, or job? Circle the personal pronouns in the answer.

Name of interviewee: _____

Topic: hobby / sport / job (circle one)

Response:

_____

_____

_____

_____

_____

_____

NAME _____   DATE _____

Subject, Object, and Possessive Pronouns

LESSON 6
NOUNS AND PRONOUNS

> The **subject** (or focus) of a sentence is always a noun or pronoun. You can find the subject by asking "Who?" or "What?" before the verb.
>
> **Example**   A notebook of ideas helps me write.
> Ask: "What helps?"   Answer: A notebook does.
> The subject is *notebook*.
>
> The **object** of a verb is the person or thing upon which the verb acts. The object of a preposition is the noun that follows it. Find the object by asking "Whom?" or "What?" after the verb or preposition.
>
> **Example**   Return this lost pen to Imelda.
>
> Ask: "Return what?"   Ask: "To whom?"
> Answer: "This pen."   Answer: Imelda.
> *Pen* is the object of the verb *return*.   *Imelda* is the object of the preposition *to*.
>
> A **possessive pronoun** refers to something that belongs to somebody.
>
> **Example**   **Where is the trophy that belongs to me?**
> **Where is mine?** (*Mine* replaces *the trophy that belongs to me.*)

Try It Out

Write the appropriate pronoun in each of the following sentences. In some sentences, more than one type of pronoun can be used.

1 My math teacher gave _____ a day's extension after my illness.

2 My neighbor and _____ have not decided who should build the new fence.

3 Our teacher wanted to know if any of _____ had read Tolkien's *The Hobbit*.

4 My picture's all right but _____ is terrific!

5 Who goes first? Tammy or _____ ?

Go Grammar! (11)

Taking It Further

1 Fill in appropriate pronouns in the following paragraph from a student's film review.

Taking a Stand looks at racial tension in a neighborhood. The TV special shows the prejudice faced by an African American family and asks _____ how _____ might behave in the same situation. The film encourages people to identify with the main characters and the few residents who reach out to _____. After watching _____ , we realized that the family's situation was similar to _____.

2 Now specify the person and number of each pronoun you inserted above and indicate whether it is a *subject*, *object*, or *possessive* form. The first one has been done for you.

Example   us: first-person plural object

_____

_____

In the Real World

Create a catchy advertisement for a popular film. Write a short heading followed by a lively sentence. Include personal pronouns in your advertisement and underline them.

Example   *At last!*
The climax to *Lord of the Rings.*
Cheer Frodo and Sam as <u>they</u> battle evil.
When will <u>you</u> see <u>it</u>?

_____

_____

_____

_____

Pronoun Agreement

NOUNS AND PRONOUNS

A pronoun should **agree** in number (singular or plural) with the noun or pronoun to which it refers.

Examples   I keep a diary and write in **it** every day. (*It* is singular and refers to *diary*, a singular noun.)

Students should do their best when **they** prepare an assignment. (*They* is plural and refers to *students*, a plural noun.)

Pronouns should also agree in **person**. Be consistent in using first, second, or third person to refer to the same people or things.

Examples   We aim to leave home at the same time so that **we** arrive at school on time. (*we* = first person plural)

Jeremy, if **you** take more time with your work, **you** will improve your performance. (*you* = second person singular)

The following **indefinite pronouns** are always singular: *each, everybody, somebody, someone, one, anyone, no one, everyone,* and *nobody.*

Examples   **Each** of the art students explained **his or her** panel before adding it to the class quilt.

Everybody needs to give **his or her** pet a little love!

Someone will have to pay for the damage **he** or **she** did to the train station.

Use the combination *he or she* to refer to an unknown individual, or rewrite the sentence to include a third-person plural pronoun (*they/them*).

Example   If a student performs poorly, he should seek advice from the teacher. (Inaccurate because the student could be either a boy or a girl.)

Singular   If a student performs poorly, **he or she** should seek advice from the teacher.

Plural   If *students perform* poorly, *they* should seek advice from the teacher.

Try It Out

1   Circle the pronouns in the following letter to the editor. Write the person and number of each pronoun on the lines below.

Please stop wasting precious water. If we waste water when taking a shower or brushing teeth, it just goes down the drain and into the ocean. Worse, if one just throws dirty water in the gutter, then you pollute local streams and rivers.

If we save water and avoid polluting it, though, we can avoid a serious shortage in the future and keep the environment healthy.

K. Poole, 7th Grade

_____

_____

2   Which personal pronoun is used most often in the letter? Revise the third sentence so that its pronouns match the personal pronoun used most often.

_____

_____

_____

Taking It Further

In your notebook, write a letter supporting or opposing the above view of water use. Make sure your pronouns are consistent in person and number.

In the Real World

In your local newspaper, find a letter to the editor that raises an issue of personal interest. Cut it out and paste it below. Write a summary of the letter in no more than 30 words. Make sure you use pronouns consistently.

Paste Here

_____

_____

_____

_____

REVISION TEST 1   Nouns and Pronouns

Review Lessons 1–7 before completing this test.

1   Circle any nouns in the following advertisement. Above each noun, write *P* if it is a proper noun, *A* if its an abstract noun, and CL if it is a collective noun. Do not label common nouns unless they are also abstract or collective.

Witchred Restaurant

Sylvio and Maria Dino welcome you to this remarkable restaurant nestled

in the Ouachita Mountains. The atmosphere is stunning. Depending on the

season, you may see flocks of migrating geese or small herds of deer outside.

Visitors to this exquisite place will savor the fine Italian food and relax in

contentment and natural beauty.

2   Circle the personal pronouns in the following advice column. Write the appropriate label above each pronoun: S = subject pronoun, O = object pronoun, P = possessive pronoun. The first one has been done for you.

Here's some advice: Let other people talk rather than hogging the conversation.

P/S

Remember that silence is golden (yours, that is). Listen to other people's

stories. Take notice of what they tell you and learn more about them. That

way, rather than just thinking about personal experiences of yours, you can

relate to theirs.

3   Rewrite the following sentences so that the pronouns and verbs agree in person and number. Be sure that your pronouns do not exclude one gender or the other.

a   Each of the speakers explained what freedom meant to them.

_____

b   Nobody have the right to be rude to others in class.

_____

c   If a driver maintains his vehicle, then bad accidents can be avoided.

_____

d One can work hard, but you can also relax and still perform well.

_____

e A minister spends most of his weekends at church.

_____

f If anyone has questions, they should ask.

_____

g Should we turn in money that one finds on the ground?

_____

h The visitors were encouraged to write his or her name in the guest book.

_____

4 Write instructions on how to walk a dog or ride a skateboard or bike in three steps.
Include at least four nouns and two pronouns and underline them.

_____

_____

_____

_____

LESSON 8 (VERBS) Action Verbs

> An **action verb** expresses activity, whether it is physical or mental.
>
> **Examples** The squirrel **leapt** from tree to tree.
> Jane **wondered** what she would make on her exam.
>
> Verbs can enhance and enliven your writing if you choose them well. The verb *go*, for example, adds nothing of interest for the reader. On the other hand, a well-chosen verb like *dash* or *creep* can provide extra meaning and convey a vivid image as effectively as any adjective.

Try It Out

Rewrite each sentence below by replacing the verb in italics with a more effective, vivid one. Change other words as necessary.

Example Jane *went* to the bus stop. → *Jane hurried to the bus stop.*

1 The girl *walked* into the room.

_____

2 Grass *grew* on the old path.

_____

3 Vince *disliked* his upstairs neighbor.

_____

4 Dozens of butterflies *were* all over the field.

_____

5 The radio host *talked* into the microphone.

_____

Taking It Further

1 Fill in the blanks with vivid verbs. Avoid verbs like *be, do, make* and *go*.

Example The weary traveler ___*dragged*___ her luggage behind her.

Go Grammar! (17)

a Peter _____ into the principal's office.

b The exhausted runner _____ to the finishing line.

c Great Britain _____ with interesting historical sites.

d The invading army _____ the castle.

e At daybreak scores of vacationers _____ onto the beach.

f The football team _____ in the face of great opposition.

2 For each overused verb, provide five vivid alternatives of your own. Use a dictionary or a thesaurus if you like. One item has already been done for you.

Overused verb	Vivid alternatives
go	run, dawdle, rush, slouch, shuffle
say	
do	
make	
come	
walk	

In the Real World

Read the following review of a computer game.

JAK 2

If you are looking for a real adventure game, Jak and his little rabbit-friend Daxter are the guys to see. This game is colorful, noisy, and a lot of fun to play.

It actually feels like you are playing a Disney movie. The graphics are very cartoonish, and they really fit the fantasy theme of the game. You'll find yourself blasting robots, dodging obstacles as you surf around on your hoverboard, solving puzzles, and more. There's no gore, so Jak is suitable for kids; however, the story is gripping enough to grab the more mature gamer as well.

Australian Netguide. Issue 65 (October 2003). p. 71.

1 In your workbook, compose an advertisement for your favorite computer game, carefully selecting the verbs for maximum effect.

2 Discuss with a small group of your classmates (no more than four per group) the verbs you have chosen and the effectiveness of your choices.

NAME _____   DATE _____

LESSON 9 VERBS   **The Verb *Be***

The verb *be* is used as a main verb to indicate that something exists or to link the subject to words that describe or rename it.

Examples Jude **is** a terrific hockey player. (present tense)
Jude **was** a terrific hockey player in his youth. (past tense)
Jude **will be** a terrific hockey player next year. (future tense)

The verb *be* is also used as a helping verb. When a form of *be* is combined with a present participle (a verb ending in *-ing*, such as *running*), it indicates a continuing action.

Examples She **is running** away.
He **was walking** to the museum but changed his mind.

Try It Out

1 Write the appropriate form of the verb *be* in each column below.

	Person	Singular	Plural
Present	1st	I	we
	2nd	you	you
	3rd	he/she/it	they
Past	1st	I	we
	2nd	you	you
	3rd	he/she/it	they
Future	1st	I	we
	2nd	you	you
	3rd	he/she/it	they

2 Underline the form of the verb *be* in each of the following sentences, and write its tense on the line provided.

Example He is training for the finals. ___present___

a They will be at the movies on Friday. _____

b Our first choice is to skip the concert. _____

c The truck was sliding down the slope. _____

Go Grammar! 19

NAME _____   **DATE** _____

   d You are a kind person. _____

   e We were an hour late for the wedding. _____

Taking It Further

1 Identify how the form of the verb *be* is used in each of the following sentences. If it is a main verb, write M on the line provided. If it is a helping verb, write H and underline the main verb.

  Example   George **was** <u>playing</u> in the game. __H__

   a Michelle **was** sad after she heard the news. _____

   b Charlie **is** buying a car tomorrow. _____

   c Jason **is** a real character. _____

   d I **am** going to the lecture. _____

   e I **am** a good student. _____

   f The horses **were** hungry after the long trail ride. _____

   g Shingles **were** blowing off the roof. _____

   h The bus **will be** late again because of rush hour. _____

2 The verb *be* can be used in many ways, but often a more specific and vivid verb can convey your meaning more clearly and directly. In each of these sentences, replace the verb *be* and the following noun or adjective with a single verb that means the same thing.

  Example   Fay is a painter of pictures. _Fay paints pictures_

   a My backpack is a holder for many things. _____

   b Look how that dog is a follower to him. _____

   c The sky was dark during the eclipse. _____

   d I am excellent at cooking. _____

   e This book will be inspiring to many readers. _____

In the Real World

You are going to introduce a guest speaker at a school assembly. Decide who the speaker is and what he or she will be speaking about. Write your introduction in your notebook. Then, locate all the places where you have used forms of the verb *be*. Underline the form of *be* if you have used it as a helping verb, and circle it if you have used it as a main verb.

(20) **Go Grammar!**

© Harcourt Achieve Inc. All rights reserved.

LESSON (10) Verb Forms and Verb Phrases
VERBS

Verbs tell when an action happens — in the past, present, or future.

Examples   I **watch** the game. (present tense)
You **watched** the game yesterday. (past tense)
He **will watch** the game tomorrow. (future tense)

Each verb has four basic forms: the **base form,** the **present participle,** the **past,** and the **past participle.**

Examples

Base Form	Present Particple	Past	Past Participle
climb	climbing	climbed	climbed
hear	hearing	heard	heard
do	doing	did	done

The **present participle** is formed by adding -ing to the base form.

Example   I am listen**ing** to you.

Past participles can be regular or irregular.

• For regular verbs, add -ed to the infinitive.

Example   I listen**ed** to you.

• Some irregular verbs change the vowel sound.

Example   I **run** to the gate. → I **ran** to the gate.

• Other irregular verbs have the same form for the present, past, and past participle.

Example   Wait while I **put** these bags down. (present)
She **put** the groceries on the counter. (past)
The Browns had **put** a hat on their snowman. (past participle)

Verb phrases are formed by using a helping verb with a present or past participle (see Lesson 9) or with the base form. The most common helping verbs are *be, do, have, will, should, could, would,* and *can.*

> **Examples** I **am skating** as fast as I can. (*be* + present participle)
> She **has skated** before. (*have* + past participle)
> You **should skate** more often. (*should* + base form)

1   Fill in the table below with the correct base, present participle, past, or past participle form of each verb.

Base Form	Present participle	Past	Past participle
go	going	went	gone
stop		stopped	stopped
command			
		admired	
			kicked
ring	ringing		
get			
	bending		
		burst	
catch			
meet			
	reading		
be			
buy			
lead			

2   For each sentence, underline the main verb and circle any helping verbs. Then, on the line provided, identify whether the main verb is in *base, present participle, past,* or *past participle* form.

Example   I ⟨have⟩ seen him. _past participle_____

a   The grandparents are enjoying the school play. _____

b   The blaze destroyed the building. _____

   c Greta has left her purse behind. _____

   d I will go to the grocery store with you. _____

   e The storm lasted for a week. _____

   f The girls can collect empty milk jugs for the lab. _____

   g Sarah brought her basketball. _____

   h The horse had lost a shoe. _____

Taking It Further

1 In addition to being used as main verbs, participles can appear by themselves in descriptive phrases. For each sentence, underline any participles that are not main verbs.

   Example   <u>Wrestling</u> with the keys, she struggled to open the door.

   a Screaming, the excited fans greeted the band.

   b He galloped across the field, standing in the stirrups.

   c Bitten by mosquitoes, we dove into the tent for cover.

   d They were sitting outside the principal's office, considering their punishment.

   e The walls, repainted several times and now peeling, have seen better days.

2 Underline the verb phrase(s) in each of the following sentences. Then, write the tense of the helping verb (H) and the form of the main verb (M) on the line provided.

   Example   Exhausted, they <u>had slept</u> for twelve hours. _<u>H past, M past part.</u>_

   a Jack has carried the canoe by himself. _____

   b Sophie does like her French class. _____

   c He was chosen for his ability to kick goals. _____

   d Drivers are becoming frustrated with the detour. _____

   e They will be going to band practice after they have finished here.

   _____

In the Real World

1 Rewrite the following passage in the past tense on the lines provided.

> And so one day . . . an acquaintance tells him of a sure thing — a house near Soho Square that is known to be full of silver . . . . On a moonless night, the three youths creep in through a window . . . and start piling silver chocolate-pots and plates into a burlap sack. They leave by the same window, but this time, silver clinking, they attract the attention of a passerby . . . . The man confronts the robbers; a rickety pistol is drawn, and in the scuffle the man is shot. Dropping the bag of silver, the three flee the scene, but the damage has been done.
>
> *Con Men and Cutpurses* by Lucy Moore. Harmondsworth: Penguin, 2000. pp. xviii-xix.

_____

_____

_____

_____

_____

_____

_____

2 What is the effect of changing the tense?

_____

_____

3 What ideas has this given you about your own writing?

_____

_____

_____

NAME _____   DATE _____

 **LESSON 11** VERBS **Subject and Predicate**

Sentences are composed of two parts: subject and predicate. The **subject** is the topic of the sentence. The **predicate,** which contains the verb, is what is said about the subject.

Example   The happy children played a game of hide-and-seek.
              subject   *predicate*

The same thought can be expressed in a different way. Notice that in the new example below, the subject (or the doers) of the original sentence is now in the predicate. The verb in this new sentence is in **passive voice.**

Example   A game of hide-and-seek was played by the happy children.
              subject   *predicate*

Try It Out

Underline the predicate and circle the subject in each of the following sentences.

Example   Wolves are howling in the distance.

1   George is in the gym.

2   The house disappeared in the flood.

3   A stray dog trotted casually across the park.

4   The workers were paid on Friday.

5   Three of us visited the art gallery.

6   The surfer paddled madly to get over the swell.

7   My friend Mark saw her yesterday in the shopping center.

8   A good time was had by all.

9   In the middle of the garden grew an ancient tree.

10   Would you mind trading places with me?

Taking It Further

Fill in the blanks with an appropriate subject (in red pen) or predicate (in blue pen).

Example   The orchestra _played in the new concert hall. (blue)_

1 Martin _____.

2 _____ played in Saturday's soccer match.

3 The skateboarders _____.

4 _____ were taken by the detectives.

5 The dog with the curly coat _____.

6 _____ danced with the girls from their sister school.

7 _____ ran to the bus stop in the rain.

8 The plane _____.

9 _____ worked at Macca's Restaurant part-time.

10 The basketball team _____.

In the Real World

1 Circle the subjects and underline the predicates in the passage below. You do not need to underline connecting words like *and*, *although*, and *as though*.

> I remember it well, although I was only five at the time. We visited him as he stood on the stone ramparts of his tower, right in the middle of the lake. His lean figure strutted this way and that, and with his left hand he stroked his waxed moustache, some would say nervously, as though even then he could detect any wavering in our attention, without so much as a glance in our direction. An awestruck silence would sweep over the entire assembly. Only then did he turn to address us. And what an unforgettable experience it was.
>
> "The Preacher in the Tower" by Raimondo Cortese, in *The Penguin Century of Australian Short Stories*, C. Bird, ed. Harmondsworth: Penguin, 2000. p. 808.

2 Identify with a classmate any sentences that have more than one subject and predicate. What is the effect of having multiple subjects and predicates in the same sentence?

_____

_____

_____

REVISION TEST 2 Verbs

Review Lessons 8–11 before completing this test.

1 Underline the verb or verb phrase in each sentence.

  a Peter plays at the stadium regularly.

  b I will sing in the concert on Tuesday.

  c A swarm of wasps chased the unfortunate dog.

  d Emma is jogging two miles a day now.

  e After the storm the sun has shone at last.

  f The kangaroo leapt from the rocks.

  g You should see the funny pictures in this book.

  h There will be time to talk later.

  i Here stands a beautiful monument to the fallen.

  j Do you ever miss your home?

2 Select the most appropriate verb from the box to complete the sentences.

screeched	creaked	gushed	crashed	shouted
rattled	fled	pinched	whispered	sizzled
steamed	lapped	scratched	squeaked	rumbled

  a The oil _____ in the old pan.

  b The thief _____ from the crime scene.

  c When she opened it, the rusty gate _____ .

  d The waves _____ at the edge of the rock pool.

  e The old cannon _____ over the cobblestones.

  f Soaring overhead, the hawk _____ as it hunted.

  g Laurie's fashionable shoes _____ her toes with every step.

  h Thunder _____ across the open plain.

  i A kettle _____ on the wood-burning stove.

  j Water _____ from the broken hydrant and flooded the street.

3 Select a vivid verb to replace the overused forms of
go in parentheses.

a The lawn mower (went) _____ at the first tug of the cord.

b The bell (goes off) _____ at the end of each period.

c Our guest speaker (went on) _____ speaking for over an hour.

d A line of hikers (went up) _____ the steep path.

e The hungry lions are (going after) _____ the zebras.

f The students (went back) _____ to school in August.

g Adults must (go with) _____ any children who want to see the movie.

h The dynamite (went off) _____ in the mine shaft.

i Curious visitors (went through) _____ the famous house.

j The song (goes) _____ a little like this.

4 On the line provided, identify the form of each underlined verb as *base, present participle,
past,* or *past participle.*

a The first mate rang the ship's bell at noon. _____

b The farmer will shear his sheep today. _____

c He has ridden in five bicycle races so far. _____

d Marco is leaving at eight o'clock this morning. _____

e The rowboat quickly sank in the lake. _____

f We have built a tree house for my little sister. _____

g How brightly the stars are shining tonight! _____

h Must we show all of our work for each math problem? _____

i Simon lay behind a rock with his camera ready. _____

j Schools of jellyfish swam alongside the ferry. _____

5 Underline the predicate in each sentence.

a George is a good cook.

b None of us believed Lisa's story at first.

c Hundreds were saved thanks to the firefighters' quick response.

d My cousin Sarah is a rude child.

e Did you move my folder somewhere?

f At camp the whole group sang the same old songs.

LESSON 12 **Adjectives**
ADJECTIVES
AND ADVERBS

> An **adjective** is a word that describes a noun or pronoun.
>
> **Examples** She wore a **tiny** hat. (The adjective *tiny* describes the appearance of the hat.)
> We met the **seven** sailors. (The adjective *seven* indicates how many sailors there were.)
>
> In the passage below, you can see how the adjectives work to describe the nouns.
>
> > Papa, as the **little** ones called him, was **old** and **bent**. His **cramped one-room** house hid behind the **thick green** hedge that ringed the **paved** schoolyard. He greeted **every** child with a **bright** smile and an **kind** word.

Try It Out

1   Write suitable adjectives to go with these nouns.

a _____ baby   f _____ castle

b _____ wolf   g _____ bush

c _____ house   h _____ surfer

d _____ ship   i _____ storm

e _____ soil   j _____ clothes

2   Underline each adjective and circle the noun that it describes.

Example   He truly is a <u>terrible</u> singer.

a   He was a courageous soldier.

b   The biker was very helpful.

c   Georgie is a lively little girl.

d   The tiny seahorse attached itself to a long strand of seaweed.

e   The church bell rang out clearly in the still summer morning.

Go Grammar! 29

Taking It Further

1 An antonym is a word opposite in meaning to another word (see Lesson 29). Provide antonyms for the following adjectives. Do not use the prefixes un- or in-.

Example shallow _deep_____

happy	inferior
wise	proud
false	smooth
mean	wild

2 Change these nouns into adjectives.

Example pride _proud_____

innocence	heat
taste	danger
value	doubt
courtesy	awe

3 Change these verbs into adjectives.

Example talk _talkative_____

love	inquire
differ	quarrel
terrify	value

In the Real World

Underline the adjectives in the following real estate listing. Can you replace them with more interesting and attractive ones? Rewrite the passage on a separate page.

Do-it-yourselfer's Delight!
Classic family home in need of love and care. Includes four small but bright bedrooms, large dining area, and a pretty fireplace. Features an old-looking master bathroom and a decent kitchen. The planted yard will be popular with children and pets. Live in a nice area close to shops and public transportation.

NAME _____   DATE _____

 **LESSON 13**
ADJECTIVES
AND ADVERBS

Comparison of Adjectives

Adjectives add meaning to nouns or pronouns and can be used to compare two or more things. They are used in the **positive, comparative,** and **superlative** degrees according to how many nouns or pronouns they describe.

Example   This is a **big** house. (positive; describes one thing)
This house is **bigger** than that one (comparative; compares two things)
This is the **biggest** house I have ever seen (superlative; compares more than two things)

Note that if the adjective is a short word (one or two syllables), you can often simply add *-er* (comparative) or *-est* (superlative). If the word is longer, then use *more* or *most*.

Regular Comparisons		
Positive	**Comparative**	**Superlative**
small	smaller	smallest
happy	happier	happiest
beautiful	more beautiful	most beautiful

Irregular Comparisons		
Positive	**Comparative**	**Superlative**
good	better	best
well	better	best
bad	worse	worst
little (amount)	less	least
much	more	most
many	more	most

Try It Out

1   Complete the following sentences by writing the comparative form of the adjective in parentheses.

Example   He was (fast) _____*faster*_____ than his opponents.

a Michael was the (sweet) _____ of the twins.

b We were (late) _____ than the others.

c I had never seen (mountainous) _____ country.

d James feels (bad) _____ than he did yesterday.

e The rescuers were (courageous) _____ than we had realized.

2   Complete the sentences by writing the superlative form of the adjective in parentheses.

a The (old) _____ man at the reunion was 103.

b Adam was the (happy) _____ baby in the nursery.

c They were the (talented) _____ musicians in the school.

d We had the (much) _____ fun ever at the fall festival.

e The paper featured five of the year's (interesting) _____ stories.

Taking It Further

1   On the line provided indicate whether the underlined adjective is in the positive, comparative, or superlative degree.

Example   My right wrist is the <u>weaker</u> one. _____ Comparative _____

a Jason was the louder of the two children. _____

b The most intelligent girl in the class is Sarah. _____

c It was one ugly dog. _____

d Jake was the more talkative of the couple. _____

e This is the worst drought we've had in years. _____

In the Real World

Create a dialogue between two sports commentators, discussing the merits of two teams. Use comparative/superlative adjectives, including *stubborn, tough, talented, persistent, showy.*

_____

_____

_____

NAME _____   DATE _____

LESSON 14 Adverbs

ADJECTIVES AND ADVERBS

An **adverb** tells us more about a verb, adjective, or another adverb. Adverbs indicate how (manner), when (time), where (place), or to what extent (degree) something happened.

Examples   The boy ran **slowly**. (how/manner)
We will go **tomorrow**. (when/time)
She searched **everywhere**. (where/place)
The room was **more** lavish than any they had seen before.
(to what extent/degree)

Most adverbs, like adjectives, have three degrees of comparison: positive, comparative, and superlative.

Examples   He ate **fast,** but she ate **faster** than he. They ate **fastest** of all.

Try It Out

Complete the following sentences by adding appropriate adverbs.

Example   The thief ran _____desperately_____ from the police.

1   The skier cheered _____ as she reached the bottom of the run.

2   The children listened _____ to the fairytale.

3   The overloaded truck rolled _____ down the gravel road.

4   Smoke curled _____ from the camp fire.

5   The kite spiraled _____ to the ground.

Taking It Further

1   Many adverbs can be formed simply by adding -ly to an adjective. Form adverbs from the following adjectives by adding -ly.

Adjective	Adverb	Adjective	Adverb
careful	carefully	immediate	
free		funny	
true		final	

Go Grammar!   33

2 Some adverbs do not end in -ly. These include adverbs of time (such as *soon, yesterday, later*), adverbs of place (such as *everywhere, somewhere*), and adverbs of degree (such as *most, quite, so*). For each of the following sentences, add an adverb as indicated in parentheses.

Example   She was _____*most*_____ unhappy about the mix-up. (degree)

a My ferret is _____ intelligent. (degree)

b Out of the entire class he answered the questions _____ easily. (degree)

c He ran _____ past the entrance. (manner)

d I am _____ glad you were able to come. (degree)

e Simone will visit her grandmother _____. (time)

f You can leave the bowling ball _____. (place)

g The presenter spoke _____ loudly than they were used to. (degree)

h Nick's junk was scattered _____ in the room. (place)

i The winners were _____ lucky people. (degree)

j Could we fold the laundry _____? (time)

3 Write the comparative and superlative forms of the following adverbs.

Positive	Comparative	Superlative
slowly	more slowly	most slowly
fast		
well		
badly		
little		

In the Real World

On a separate page, rewrite the following passage, adding appropriate adverbs and adjectives. What is the effect of adding these words?

The figure appeared over the ridge. It grew from a spot on the horizon to a blot on the snow. Behind it followed the family: a woman holding what looked like a package, a child disappearing at intervals in the drifts, and dogs pulling a sled. As I waited for them to cross the ford in the river, I began to wonder where they had come from and why they had come here at all. I had nothing to give them in the way of food, and they knew it. Perhaps their journey needed a destination.

REVISION TEST ③ Adjectives and Adverbs

Review Lessons 12–14 before completing this test.

1 Change the following nouns and verbs into adjectives. Then, use each of them appropriately in a sentence. Do not use any -*ing* endings.

a innocence _____

_____

b robot _____

_____

c pain _____

_____

d flex _____

_____

e diplomat _____

_____

g appear _____

_____

h option _____

_____

2 Change the following adjectives into adverbs and use each of them appropriately in a sentence.

a lazy _____

_____

b humble _____

_____

c shrill _____

_____

d timid _____

_____

e skillful _____

_____

f handsome _____

_____

g full _____

_____

h fortunate _____

_____

3 Provide the comparative and superlative forms of the following adjectives.

Positive	Comparative	Superlative	Positive	Comparative	Superlative
large			good		
beautiful			old		
bad			ugly		

4 Provide the comparative and superlative forms of the following adverbs.

Positive	Comparative	Superlative	Positive	Comparative	Superlative
fast			quickly		
loudly			badly		
much			well		

5 Underline the adjectives and circle the adverbs in each of the following sentences.

a Dale and Christa stared blankly at the television.

b Could you order me a large salad?

c The elderly lady shuffled wearily across the busy road.

d Because it's Sunday, the downtown stores close early.

e The champion football team played so hard that they were limping by the end of the third game.

NAME _____   DATE _____

LESSON 15
PREPOSITIONS
AND
CONJUNCTIONS

Prepositions

> **Prepositions** indicate the position of one person or thing in relation to another.
> Common prepositions include the following.
>
> | by | from | between | over | of | against | among | except | with |
> | to | inside | at | towards | in | into | for | without | on | beneath |
>
> **Examples** Claudio's car was parked **below** the building.
> The skateboard park is **behind** the bus depot.
> Moira stayed at the party **until** midnight.

Try It Out

Complete each of the following sentences with an appropriate preposition.

1 _____ dawn three rabbits scurried _____ the lawn.

2 _____ the bridge we noticed a pile _____ trash.

3 The teacher sat _____ the two students _____ the assembly.

4 _____ the rain, the children resumed their stickball match _____ the street.

5 The music was played _____ an orchestra hidden _____ some scenery.

6 Wayne parks his car _____ the garage to leave space _____ his motorcycle.

7 Tracy backed away _____ the ferocious dog as it barked _____ her.

8 We were surprised how many people _____ our block care _____ the environment.

9 Most _____ the students in the class don't care _____ historical movies.

10 Leon jumped _____ the diving board and _____ the pool.

Taking It Further

1 Write instructions on how to get to your classroom from the school's main entrance. Use as many of the following prepositions as possible.

about	down	inside	without	through
beneath	into	toward	across	up

_____

_____

_____

_____

2 Finish each sentence by adding appropriate prepositions and other words.

Example   The student went ___*into the shop and bought a magazine*___.

a We hiked _____.

b The girls looked _____.

c I listened _____.

d _____ spectacular fireworks exploded.

e _____ lived an enchanted salamander.

In the Real World

Find a short article in a local newspaper. Staple it to this page and circle all the prepositions you can find.

Example   Hand-made furniture carved from recycled wood has become increasingly popular. Tom Wainwright of Natural Interiors is having trouble keeping up with demand. "I'm looking at hiring more staff," he said, "but I'm very particular about the standard of work that comes from my workshop, and it's hard to find committed apprentices."

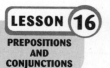

Conjunctions

LESSON 16
PREPOSITIONS
AND
CONJUNCTIONS

Conjunctions join words, phrases, and clauses in a meaningful way. A clause is any group of words that has a subject and a verb.

Coordinating conjunctions join words, phrases, or clauses that have equal status. Here is a list of the most common coordinating conjunctions.

and	but	or	nor	for	so	yet
both . . . and		either . . . or		neither . . . nor		

Examples   fish **or** chicken

both a faithful friend **and** a thoughtful critic

The workers went on strike for one day, **but** they returned to work after receiving news that no more jobs would be lost.

Subordinating conjunctions join clauses that do not have equal status. The idea in one clause is less important than (subordinate to) the other. The clause expressing the less important idea is called a **subordinate clause,** while the one expressing the main idea is called a **main clause**.

Subordinating conjunctions include the following.

after	although	as	because	before	for	if
now	since	unless	until	when	where	whether	while

In each case, the main clause can stand alone, but the subordinate clause cannot.

I read the whole book // **because** I wanted to find out the ending.

main clause   *subordinate clause*

Try It Out

Join the following pairs of sentences into one sentence. You can delete words in the second sentence and add a coordinating conjunction, or you can add a subordinating conjunction. Change the punctuation and capitalization as necessary.

Example   The scouts hiked for three days. They stopped for meals at the same time each day. → **The scouts hiked for three days and stopped for meals at the same time each day.**

1   My parents spoke to me. They had a conference with my teacher.

_____

2 Katrina is the better dancer. The other girl is very talented.

_____

3 The telephone will ring. Somebody in the office answers it.

_____

4 Do you want to store the leftovers? Do you want to help wash the dishes?

_____

Taking It Further

Using conjunctions, join these simple sentences into a total of three or four sentences.

The fighter jet was on fire. It roared over the airfield. There was nothing the ground crew could do. Onlookers waited for the worst. A huge explosion was heard on the vacant playing fields. Then, a white parachute could be seen floating to earth.

_____

_____

_____

_____

In the Real World

1 Underline the coordinating conjunctions in the following passage.

I lowered my *Times* and stole a glance at his face. I suppose he was about the same age as me — sixty-two or three — but he had one of those unpleasantly handsome, brown, leathery countenances that you see nowadays in advertisements for men's shirts — the lion shooter and the polo player and the Everest climber and the tropical explorer and the racing yachtsman all rolled into one.... Personally, I mistrust all handsome men. The superficial pleasures of this life come too easily to them, and they seem to walk the world as though they themselves were personally responsible for their good looks.

Someone Like You by Roald Dahl. Harmondsworth: Penguin, 1970. p. 188.

2 How many coordinating conjunctions are used in the passage above? _____

3 What is the effect of using so many conjunctions? Discuss with a classmate.

REVISION TEST 4 # Prepositions and Conjunctions

Review Lessons 15–16 before completing this test.

1 Underline the prepositions in the following sentences.

   a A choir sang the national anthem before the game.

   b Neither girl spoke to me afterwards.

   c Daniel will wait outside the bank, but not for long.

   d The tennis player hit a serve over the net, but it was called out.

   e She rode through the desert on a horse with brown markings.

   f The policeman fell against his car yet managed to stay on his feet.

   g In the country, people are friendly to one another when approached.

   h The nurse received awards both for her bravery throughout the war and for her community service after it.

2 Underline the prepositions in the following passage.

Across the stadium, I could see the huge band of Rollingwood supporters in the visitor seats. I sat between an elderly lady and a teenager throughout the game. They stood up and screamed with each goal scored by Rollingwood. After the half-time break, I had a headache.

3 Underline the *coordinating* conjunctions in the following passage.

Diamonds and pearls are considered anyone's best friend. They have long been valued as much as gold or silver. For centuries people have dug deep into the earth for diamonds and searched under the sea where the oyster hides its riches.

4 Underline the *subordinating* conjunctions in the following passage.

After the snow fell, everyone in the neighborhood was happy. People played in the snow before they had breakfast. A toddler and her parents built a snowman, but it soon melted in the midday sun. Although the "white stuff" did not last, it made the whole day magical.

5 Write a set of instructions on how to videotape a television program or set an alarm clock. Include at least four prepositions and four conjunctions.

_____

_____

_____

_____

_____

6 Join the following pairs of sentences into one sentence. You can delete words in the second sentence and add a coordinating conjunction, or you can add a subordinating conjunction. Change capitalization and punctuation as necessary.

a You can buy the cheaper model now. You can save up for a nicer one.

_____

b The current economic problems are particularly serious. The economy is always a cause for concern.

_____

_____

c The police officer turned on her lights. She wanted to pull over a speeding motorcyclist.

_____

_____

d The pirates searched everywhere on the island for the missing treasure. Lack of food and water forced them to leave.

_____

_____

NAME _____   DATE _____

LESSON 17   PREFIXES AND SUFFIXES

Prefixes

Prefixes are word parts placed before other words to change their meanings. Prefixes have come into English from Old English, French, Greek, and Latin.

Negative prefixes change the meaning of a word to its antonym (opposite). For example, the Latin *dis-*, meaning "not" changes *like* to *dislike* (not like). Other negative prefixes include *non-*, *de-*, *mis-*, and *un-*.

Some common Latin prefixes

Prefix	Meaning	Examples
bi-	two	biennial, bicycle, bisect
co-, com-	with	cooperate, combine
ex-	out, former	extract, expel, ex-president
mis-	wrong	mislead, mistake

Some common Greek prefixes

Prefix	Meaning	Examples
anti-	against	antiseptic, antidote
auto-	self	automatic, automobile
micro-	small	microcosm, microscope
peri-	around	periscope, perimeter
tele-	far, distant	telephone, telescope

Try It Out

Write the meanings of the following prefixes in the table below. Then, write two other words that include that prefix. The first one has been done for you as an example.

Prefix	Meaning	Word 1	Word 2
anti-	against	antibiotic	antisocial
bi-			
co-, com-			

Go Grammar! 43

Prefix	Meaning	Word 1	Word 2
ex-	out, former		
mis-	wrong		
auto-	self		
tele-	far, distant		

Taking It Further

1   Provide a word with a prefix for each definition. The prefix does not need to come from the list in this lesson.

Example   to go completely around (verb) _____

a   more than human (adj.) _____

b   put off until later (v.) _____

c   against the law (adj.) _____

d   under the skin (adj.) _____

2   Create antonyms from the words below by adding either the prefix *dis-* (Latin, meaning "not") or *mis-* (Latin, meaning "wrong").

a _____ charge   b _____ approve   c _____ able   d _____ take

e _____ construe   f _____ robe   g _____ manage   h _____ spell

i _____ unite   j _____ demeanor   k _____ tasteful   l _____ guide

In the Real World

Some prefixes tell us about the number of something. For example, *bi-* means "two," so *bicycle* is a vehicle with two wheels. Look up the other prefixes that indicate number and complete the table below.

Prefix	Meaning	Word 1	Word 2
bi-	two	bicycle	
tri-	three		
quadr-	four		
pent-	five		

LESSON 18 Suffixes

PREFIXES AND SUFFIXES

A suffix is a word part that is placed at the end of a word to change its meaning or part of speech. Suffixes help us to identify parts of speech.

Example   *critic* (noun) + *-al* (suffix) becomes *critical* (adjective)

Common suffixes used to create **nouns**:

-er	singer	*-ness*	madness
-hood	childhood	*-ship*	kinship
-ist	physicist	*-tion*	anticipation
-ment	postponement	*-ty*	certainty

Common suffixes used to create **verbs**:

-ify	modify
-ize	mobilize

Common suffixes used to create **adjectives**:

-able	acceptable	*-less*	helpless
-ful	mindful	*-like*	childlike
-ish	stylish	*-ous*	generous

Common suffixes used to create **adverbs**:

-ly	mostly
-ward, -wards	afterward

Try It Out

Add two more examples of words that include each suffix.

Suffix	Words Including Suffix
-er	player,
-hood	motherhood,
-ist	biologist,
-ment	agreement,
-ship	friendship,
-ify	beautify,

Suffix	Words Including Suffix
-able	tolerable,
-ful	meaningful,
-ous	famous,
-ly	bravely,

Taking It Further

Select four of the words you added to the table above and use each one in a sentence.

_____

_____

_____

_____

In the Real World

Write a paragraph explaining either why you admire a particular athlete or why you enjoy playing a favorite sport. Include the following words that include suffixes: *skillful, enjoyment, famous, exercise*. Underline any other words with suffixes that you use.

_____

_____

_____

_____

_____

_____

_____

_____

REVISION TEST 5 Prefixes and Suffixes

Review Lessons 17–18 before completing this test.

1 Add a prefix to change the meaning of each word.

    a The boy had gained weight because he was _____ active.

    b The creature was _____ understood.

    c The invention of the _____ chip made computers smaller.

    d Beth wants to stay home — a most _____ adventurous girl.

    e Although they were twins, the boys looked _____ similar.

2 Write two words using each prefix.

    a tele- = distant   _____

    b co-, com- = with   _____

    c anti- = against   _____

    d auto- = self   _____

    e micro- = small, minute _____

    f bi- = two   _____

3 Write a paragraph describing your favorite computer game. Include six words with prefixes. You may choose words from the box or think of your own words.

compete	cooperate	destroy	extreme	replay	nonviolent

_____

_____

_____

_____

_____

4 Write a paragraph describing your favorite place to visit. Include six words with suffixes. You may choose words from the box or think of your own words.

| stillness | peaceful | reachable | famous | entertainment |

_____

_____

_____

_____

_____

5 Underline the suffixes in the following car advertisement.

This brand-new sedan provides wonderful excitement for the motorist. You will marvel at its beautiful design and glorious engine.

6 Provide a word with a prefix for each definition.

a the area around something (n.) _____

b make something not work (v.) _____

c an error (n.) _____

d occurring very two weeks (adj.) _____

e a former head of state (n.) _____

f upset (adj.) _____

7 For each definition, write a word that includes the suffix provided.

a not certain (adj. -ful) _____

b without restraint (adv. -ly) _____

c area around where you live (n. -hood) _____

d playing in the spirit of the game (n. -ship) _____

e to move into action (v. -ize) _____

f lack of moisture (n. -ness) _____

NAME _____   DATE _____

Apostrophes in Contractions

> The apostrophe (') can be used to indicate that one or more letters have been left out of a word. Shortening a word creates a **contraction**.
>
> **Example**   Unfortunately, **I'll** have to reply that I **can't** attend the party.
>   (*I'll* = I will; *can't* = cannot)

Try It Out

1   Write out each contraction in full.

Contraction	Full word	Contraction	Full word
it's		aren't	
they'd		could've	
should've		isn't	
can't		they're	
we'll		won't	

2   Write the contracted form of each group of words.

Full word	Contraction	Full word	Contraction
I had / I would		would have	
would not		of the clock	
we have		were not	
let us		do not	
you are		was not	

Taking It Further

Each of the following sentences contains two contractions with missing apostrophes. On the line provided, rewrite each contraction using proper punctuation. Then, write out the contraction in full.

Example   I know I couldve, but I didnt! _could've — could have; didn't — did not_

1   Thats unfair — theyve gotten away with it again! _____
_____

2   Youll have to miss the contest since you didnt submit your application on time. _____
_____

3   Heres an offer you cant refuse! _____

4   Theyd have joined us if theyd known we were coming. _____
_____

5   Im not sure its the best thing to do in these circumstances. _____

6   We were so bored because itd been raining all day and the weather didnt clear. _____
_____

7   Ill taste it if youll try it first! _____

8   Suzie shouldve arrived by six oclock. _____
_____

In the Real World

Create an "Apostrophes Ready-Reference Sheet" by completing the following chart in your notebook.

Begin by writing in all of the contracted words in this lesson. Develop your Ready-Reference Sheet by writing in the contracted words used throughout your readings for class. Check your spelling and punctuation for accuracy.

Spelled Out	Contraction
I will	I'll

NAME _____   DATE _____

LESSON 20 **Apostrophes in Possessives**
PUNCTUATION

The **apostrophe** is used to show possession.
• If the noun is singular and does not end in -s, add 's.

Example   the student's assignment (the assignment belonging to the student)

• If the noun is singular and ends in -s, typically add 's.

Example   the boss's style (the style of the boss)

However, for names that have more than one syllable and that would sound awkward with an additional s sound, add only '.

Example   Odysseus' journey

• If the noun is plural and does not end in -s, add 's. If the noun is plural and ends in -s, add only '.

Examples   the women's team   the neighbors' party

Try It Out

1   Rewrite each of the following groups of words in the singular possessive form.

Example   The ball belonging to the cat _The cat's ball_____

a   The book belonging to the teacher   _____

b   The briefcase belonging to the doctor   _____

c   The price of the banana   _____

d   The house belonging to the Wilson family _____

2   Rewrite each of the following in the plural possessive form.

a   The association of the parents   _____

b   The playroom of the toddlers   _____

c   The exhibition of the artists   _____

d   The response of the writers   _____

Go Grammar!   (51)

3 Rewrite each of the following to indicate possession.

    a The bike belonging to Chris   _____

    b The club belonging to Hercules   _____

    c The friends of the women   _____

    d The pen of the sheep   _____

Taking It Further

On the line provided, correct words that are missing apostrophes of possession.

1 Several guests personal belongings were stolen during the companys party!

_____

2 Jennifers vacation was brightened by her parents generosity.

_____

3 The congregations behaviour was respectful at the politicians funeral.

_____

4 The pianists extraordinary performance held the audiences interest for over two hours.

_____

5 The sky over the birdwatchers gathering echoed with the geeses honking.

_____

6 The Joneses house will be sold in a weeks time.

_____

In the Real World

Because sports reports often contain information about the achievements of athletes and teams, their headlines often require the use of apostrophes of possession.

    Examples Martina's glory! Phillipousis' finest hour! Magpies' horror match!

Browse through the sports section in a newspaper and collect examples of headlines that use apostrophes to show possession. Cut out the examples and paste them on a separate page.

 **Periods, Question Marks, and Exclamation Points**

> **Periods** are used to
> • indicate the end of a declarative sentence (see Lesson 24)
> **Example**   Roald Dahl wrote many stories with a twist**.**
>
> • indicate that a word has been shortened (abbreviated)
> **Examples** Mr**.** Ms**.** Dr**.** Rd**.** St**.**
>
> **Question marks** are used to indicate that something has been asked or requested.
> **Example**   Are you willing to stay late today**?**
>
> **Exclamation points** are used to
> • indicate that a sentence expresses strong emotion
> **Example**   That really hurt**!**
>
> • mark **interjections**, words that show surprise or strong feeling
> **Examples** Ouch**!** Hey**!** Wow**!** Drat**!** Oh**!**

Try It Out

Place periods, question marks, and exclamation points where required in the following excerpt from the script for the play *Truth or Dare?*.

IAN: Where's Jane _____

SANDRA (*calling*): Jane _____

PETER: She's still outside _____

SANDRA: Still _____ Come in, love _____

IAN (*calling*): Jane, come in and give us a hand _____(Jane ignores him and sits on the veranda steps.)

SANDRA (*worried, to Ian*): She just refuses to come in _____ She says she won't set foot in this house _____

IAN: What _____

SANDRA: She says it's not like our old home _____

PETER: She reckons she's going to run away — all the way back across the country _____

IAN (*annoyed*): Stop being so childish, Jane _____ Grow up _____

PETER: Yeah, act your age, Jane _____

SANDRA: Why don't you just come in _____

Truth or Dare? by Laura Deriu and Noel Jordan. Unpublished, 1996.

Taking It Further

The opening of a short story must capture the reader's interest immediately. Below is the opening of Ted Ottley's story "Birthday Boy" Ottley uses a range of punctuation marks to create different types of sentences (see Lesson 24) and interest the reader.

1   Identify the punctuation in the passage below. Draw circles around periods, squares around question marks, and triangles around exclamation points.

2   Replace the punctuation marks as follows: change exclamation points to question marks; change periods to exclamation points; and change question marks to periods. Write out the passage with the new punctuation marks in your notebook.

3   Reread the passage with the new punctuation. In your notebook, explain the effects of the altered punctuation marks.

> "Jason! Will you please put that moving carton back? Now. If you don't mind!" Her voice had that desperate edge again.
>
> "C'mon Mum, I'll be late as it is."
>
> "Well, your friends will just have to wait. When the movers show up tomorrow we've got to be ready. Besides, if you'd kept track of where you'd put your things you wouldn't have had to open ten boxes to find those old shoes.'"
>
> It was only three boxes and they were his best Reeboks. Boy, could she exaggerate. Time to get out fast.
>
> "Sure, Mum," he struggled with the carton. "There — all organized. Cool?"
>
> She softened in spite of herself as he gave her a goodbye peck on the cheek. "Well, don't be too late. They're due at six in the morning. Sorry about no birthday party. Still, we can't move and entertain all at once now, can we?"
>
> "Birthday Boy" by Ted Ottley, in *Ready or Not,* M. MacLeod, ed.
> Milson's Point: Random House Australia, 1996. p. 199.

In the Real World

Working with a partner, develop the following short script. Use different types of sentences requiring periods, question marks, and exclamation points. Perform your script to the class.

A: I have something important to tell you.

B: What is it?

A: _____

B: _____

A: _____

B: _____

LESSON 22 **Commas**
PUNCTUATION

Commas are used to
- separate items in a list

Example   The study kit includes a **pencil, pen, notebook, and bookmark.**

- follow an introductory word, phrase, or clause at the beginning of a sentence

Examples   **Yes,** I did look under the cushions.
                Even though it was raining, we went camping.

- set off an explanatory phrase or clause within a sentence

Example   My grandmother**, who is 76,** won her first car race in 1960.

Commas are also used in the punctuation of direct speech (see Lesson 23).

Try It Out

Circle the commas in each sentence and indicate why they have been used.

Example   Melinda, known for her sense of humor, was the class clown.

explanatory phrase within the sentence

1   Despite our efforts to keep the surprise party secret, Mavis found out.

_____

2   Weekend activities include swimming, snorkeling, windsurfing, and fishing.

_____

3   Halt, who goes there?

_____

4   The house, which had been abandoned years ago, was bulldozed.

_____

5   Mercury, Venus, Mars, Jupiter, and Saturn were known to ancient astronomers.

_____

Go Grammar!   (55)

6 Generally speaking, you should do warm-up exercises before playing any sport.

_____

7 At last we were able to meet Rev. Park, about whom my sister had said so much.

_____

8 If you plan to go to the bank, could you stop by the post office first?

_____

Taking It Further

Place commas where appropriate in the following passage and read it to a classmate.

In general a superstition is a belief or practice that arises from a fear of the unknown. Some examples of common superstitions include beliefs that a person who breaks a mirror will get seven years' bad luck that tragedy will befall a person who walks under a ladder and that misfortune follows if a black cat crosses a person's path. Some people even keep good luck charms for example horseshoes and rabbits' feet believing that they will ward off evil.

In the Real World

In your notebook, write an informative paragraph about three superstitions. You may need to conduct some research on the topic. Use the paragraph in the previous section as a model. Include the following in your paragraph:

- a list with commas
- a sentence with an introductory word, phrase, or clause
- a sentence with additional explanatory information in the middle.

See Lessons 36 and 37 to assist you with writing your paragraph. When you are finished, reread your paragraph and complete the following checklist.

Paragraph Feature	Completed
topic sentence indicating the paragraph's focus (superstitions)	
list with commas	
sentence with an introductory word, phrase, or clause	
sentence with explanatory information in the middle	
concluding sentence	

NAME _____   DATE _____

Quotation Marks in Direct Speech

LESSON **23**
PUNCUTATION

Quotation marks are used in pairs ("") to enclose **direct speech**, the words actually spoken by a person.

Observe the following conventions when using quotation marks in direct speech.

- Enclose all the spoken words in the quotation marks.
- Begin the first word of the quotation with a capital letter.
- Use a comma to separate a phrase identifying the speaker from the quotation.
- Enclose all punctuation marks inside the quotation marks when they are part of the speaker's words (including periods, question marks, and exclamation points).
- Start a new paragraph each time the speaker changes.

Example   "Knock, knock," Megan called.
"Who's there?" Dominic asked.
She replied, "Avenue."
"Okay," he responded, "Avenue who?"
"Avenue heard this joke before?"

Try It Out

Capitalize letters and add quotation marks, commas, and end punctuation where required.

1 Gus said knock, knock   _____

Who's there asked Bryce   _____

Justin he said   _____

Justin who Bryce enquired   _____

Justin the neighborhood Gus chuckled   _____

and I thought I'd drop in   _____

2 Knock knock Peg announced   _____

Who's there Kyle asked   _____

Hatch Peg said   _____

Hatch who   _____

Bless you she giggled   _____

Go Grammar!   57

Taking It Further

Write out the following conversation from Robert Louis Stevenson's *Kidnapped* with correct punctuation and paragraph breaks.

Have you no friends said I. He said he had a father in some English seaport, I forget which. He was a fine man, too he said but he's dead. In Heaven's name cried I can you find no reputable life on shore? O, no says he, winking and looking very sly they would put me to a trade. I know a trick worth two of that, I do!

Kidnapped by Robert Louis Stevenson. Ch. 5

_____

_____

_____

_____

_____

_____

_____

Interview a family member or another student. First, brainstorm a list of questions to ask. In addition to facts about the person, your interview should provide information about his or her opinions, likes, and dislikes. Take notes during the interview, and write up the profile in dialogue form in your notebook. Check to make sure that you have punctuated direct speech correctly.

Example   Jane Court is a seventh-grade student and ballet dancer. I caught up with Jane after rehearsal.

"How long have you been involved in ballet?" I asked.

Jane looked thoughtful and answered, "Probably since I was four. That means I've been dancing for about eight years."

I asked Jane, "What do you like about ballet dancing?"

"I like dancing because it's both an individual activity and a team effort," she said. "Dancing keeps me fit, and I've made loads of friends through ballet productions."

REVISION TEST 6 # Punctuation

Review Lessons 19–23 before completing this test.

The following passages are from John Branfield's novel *Nancekuke*.

1 Read the passage below, and then answer the questions that follow it. The letters in square brackets link the questions to particular sentences.

> On the following morning was the first of the examinations. Helen did not feel too bothered about it, as they started with English Language. There was nothing to revise, and she would probably have passed it in the summer if she had not been absent.
>
> At nine o'clock [a] she was outside the examination room, [b] one of a small group shivering partly with cold and partly with nervousness. At least this time it was not held in the gym, filled with row upon row of desks. Each girl clutched a little plastic bag of pens and pencils.
>
> They shuffled their feet and hugged their arms in tight to keep warm. [c]
>
> A teacher arrived, and they went inside to find their places with their numbers. Helen arranged her things on the desk, put a heading on the answer paper, and listened to the instructions as they were read. [d] The question papers were handed out in silence. The only sounds were the rustling of paper and the teacher's [e] footsteps.
>
> She had not felt particularly anxious before, but now her heart was pounding.
>
> [f] "Open your paper and begin," [g] said the teacher.
>
> > *Nancekuke* by John Branfield. London: Gryphon Books, 1988. p. 103.

a Why has an apostrophe been used? _____

b Why has a comma been used? _____

c Why has a period been used? _____

d Why have commas been used in the previous sentence? _____

e Why has an apostrophe been used? _____

f Why have quotation marks been used? _____

g Why has a comma been used? _____

2 Rewrite the following passage on the lines provided, placing punctuation marks and capital letters in the appropriate places.

Im having the back bedroom said Alison. Ive laid claim to it. Its mine now

I have the little room said Tom

They had all gathered on the landing

where is my room, Mummy asked Paul

you wont be able to have a room each, Im afraid said Mrs Roberts. youll have to share

Im not sharing with Helen said Alison

I think that would be best. If you and Helen have the back bedroom . . .

oh no said Tom. I don't want to share with Paul. Hes a nuisance

no I think the girls ought to be together and the boys together especially as you are getting older. It will have to be that way later on, so you might as well start now. What do you think, Helen

I suppose so

Nancekuke by John Branfield. London: Gryphon Books, 1988.

_____

_____

_____

_____

_____

_____

_____

_____

_____

_____

LESSON 24
SENTENCES

Declarative and Imperative Sentences

There are four types of sentences: declarative, interrogative, imperative, and exclamatory.

A **declarative sentence** makes a statement and ends with a period.

Examples Sydney is a spectacular city.

Note that like all types of sentences, a declarative sentence must be able to stand on its own as a complete thought.

An **imperative sentence** gives a command or makes a request. Imperative sentences often begin with a verb and end with a period or an exclamation point. In the examples below, the understood subject is the pronoun *you*.

Examples **Walk** carefully across the road.
Come here right now!

Try It Out

1 For each imperative sentence below, write a declarative sentence that makes a statement about the command given in the imperative.

Example: Fire at will. → _____

a Get your *Daily Herald* here!

_____

b Hold this for me, please.

_____

c Check your tickets.

_____

d Fold your arms and watch me.

_____

2 For each declarative sentence below, write an imperative sentence that expresses the same idea as a command.

Example: Tom reminded me to lock up my bike → _____

a I told them to use the handrail when walking up the narrow path.

_____

b The policeman yelled to the jay walkers to get off the road.

_____

c The cashier politely asked us to pay at the counter.

_____

d The referee shouted at the offending player to leave the field for playing rough.

_____

Taking It Further

1 In the following passage, circle the declarative sentences and underline the imperative sentences. Do not include phrases identifying the speaker.

"You are my honored guest this evening in my humble mansion," purred Victor.

"I cannot possibly stay," Desdemona replied. "Do not trouble yourself, Count."

"No, no, I insist. Treat it as if it were your own home."

2 Now write a dialogue that includes four imperative sentences and two declarative sentences, showing what happens to the evil Count Victor.

_____

_____

_____

_____

_____

_____

_____

3 Rewrite the following paragraph so the information is given in imperative sentences rather than declarative sentences. Number each instruction. The first two have been done for you.

First you slice the bun in half. Then, you can lay a bed of lettuce on top. Next you place the sizzling burger straight onto one of the bun halves. Then, you can pile on whatever toppings you like. You should include ketchup and mustard for that authentic hamburger taste. Finally, you should put the other half of the bun on top just before you eat.

1   Slice the bun in half.

2   Lay a bed of lettuce on top.

3   _____

4   _____

5   _____

6   _____

In the Real World

1 Read the following passage carefully. Circle the imperative sentences and underline the declarative sentences.

Paragraph 1

"Dad!" I yelled. "Show 'em how it's done!' My dad is a champion lumberjack. For this event, he had to scurry up a 65-foot tree trunk using a sling around his waist and spurs at his ankles. My old man didn't pay any notice to anything around him. He stood still checking his equipment, and a hush spread over the whole crowd. Then, the referee hollered, "Start climbing!"

2 Continue the story below in two paragraphs. Include at least two imperative sentences and two declarative sentences in each paragraph.

Paragraph 2

_____

_____

_____

_____

_____

_____

_____

Paragraph 3

_____

_____

_____

_____

_____

_____

3   First write a typical imperative sentence for each of the people listed below. Then, write a declarative sentence as your reply. Try to be witty and original.

Example   Bully: Give me your lunch money. (imperative)
              Reply: You don't need to eat an extra lunch today. (declarative)

a   School photographer: _____

    Reply: _____

b   Best friend: _____

    Reply: _____

c   Parent or guardian: _____

    Reply: _____

d   Museum guard: _____

    Reply: _____

e   Bus driver: _____

    Reply: _____

f   Music or drama teacher: _____

    Reply: _____

LESSON 25 **SENTENCES**

Stringy Sentences and Semicolons

A sentence should focus on one main idea. When writers run a number of sentences together, the result is a stringy sentence that may confuse readers.

Example I awoke this morning at 9 a.m. and realized I would be late to school, so I hurried to the bus and just missed it, and I arrived at school so late that I got a detention.

To revise a stringy sentence, you need to decide how to break it into two or more sentences. Remember to begin each new sentence with a capital letter.

Revised I awoke this morning at 9 a.m. and realized I would be late to school. I hurried to the bus and just missed it. I arrived at school so late that I got a detention.

A semicolon can also be used to break up stringy sentences. The semicolon is used between two closely related sentences that are not joined by a conjunction such as *and* or *but*.

Example The roads were iced over, so we had a snow day.

Revised The roads were iced over; we had a snow day.

Try It Out

1   Revise each stringy sentence by rewriting it in shorter sentences.

   a When I checked my locker, my computer was missing, and a boy had been seen earlier standing around looking suspicious, and later he had a computer slung over his shoulder.

   _____

   _____

   _____

   _____

b When the traffic light turned red, two cars sped through the intersection, but luckily another car from the other direction slowed down, so fortunately no one was injured.

_____

_____

_____

2   Revise this stringy sentence by adding a semicolon to separate clauses (see Lesson 28) and emphasize the connection between ideas.

The coach finally sent Jeremy in because he had been sitting on the bench for the entire game, but his chance had come at last.

_____

_____

Taking It Further

Revise this stringy sentence by rewriting it in shorter sentences.

My favorite activity in summer is to snorkel around the large rock pools, and I try to find exotic fish and delicate sea-shells, but my best friend likes to snooze on the sand under a huge beach umbrella, and his sister prefers to surf the big waves, so what is your favorite summer activity?

_____

_____

_____

_____

In the Real World

In your notebook, write a song that has no punctuation and contains stringy sentences. Swap songs with a partner and rewrite them in simple sentences with proper punctuation.

 **Sentence Fragments and Dangling Modifiers**

> A **sentence fragment** is a set of words that is punctuated to look like a sentence but is not grammatically complete. The following word groups are not sentences. They lack a verb or a subject and do not express a complete idea.
>
> **Example**   Another day. Pretty boring.
>
> Some professional writers use sentence fragments for dramatic effect. Doing so can be appropriate in play scripts, poetry, novels, and stories. In most writing, however, you should avoid sentence fragments because they can be confusing and may appear to result from carelessness.
>
> **Dangling modifiers** occur when a group of words beginning a sentence does not accurately refer to what follows.
>
> **Example**   **Looking at the horizon,** the sun began its descent. (Is the sun looking at the horizon?)
>
> Here are two less confusing versions of the sentence. Notice that in each case, it is clear who looked at the horizon.
>
> **Revised**   Looking at the horizon, **I** watched the sun begin its descent.
> While **I** looked at the horizon, the sun began its descent.

Try It Out

1   Rewrite each of the following sentence fragments as a grammatically complete sentence that expresses the same basic meaning as the fragments.

   Example   Oh, not another loss for our team! Failure. Next season, then.

   Our team lost again, so we can only look forward to next season.
   _____

   a Dozens of birds. Singing in the trees.

   _____

   b A busy day! How much more to do? A dog's life.

   _____

2 Rewrite these sentences to make them clearer.

a Driving to the movies, there was a lot of traffic on the road.

_____

b Being forced to close, the nursing home residents had to find somewhere else to live.

_____

_____

Taking It Further

In the passage below, first circle the dangling modifiers. Then, on the lines provided, rewrite the paragraph so that it is clear and precise.

> Dancing on the patio of the tropical resort, a monkey climbed down a nearby vine. Suddenly performing tricks, we were startled and delighted. Some of the party guests laughed at this unexpected visitor. Eventually dancing again, the monkey's fun and games were ignored.

_____

_____

_____

_____

In the Real World

Advertisements often promote products by using sentence fragments. Find two advertisements that contain sentence fragments, and rewrite the advertisements in complete sentences below.

Example   Kangaroo sportswear. The real deal.

_____

_____

Why do you think sentence fragments make effective slogans for advertising?

_____

LESSON 27 Phrases
SENTENCES

A **phrase** is a group of words within a sentence. Phrases add information to a sentence and cannot stand alone. A phrase can serve as a noun, an adjective, or an adverb.

A phrase often starts with a preposition such as *above, at, despite, of, under, since,* or *between* (see Lesson 15).

Examples   We look forward to **seeing the old cabin again.**
(noun phrase object of the preposition *to*)

For several years, Tom has hosted Thanksgiving dinner.
(adverb phrase that tells *how long* Tom has hosted)

The farmers **of our county** have watered their crops less this season. (adjective phrase that describes *which* farmers)

A phrase can also start with a participle (see Lesson 10).

Example   **Watching carefully,** she walked along the dark corridor.
(adjective phrase that describes the pronoun *she*)

A phrase can also rename or provide extra information about a noun.

Example   **Young and impulsive**, Juliet fell in love with Romeo, **a member of an opposing family**. (*Young and impulsive* is an adjective phrase that describes Juliet. The word group *a member of an opposing family* is a noun phrase that tells something about Romeo.)

Try It Out

Underline and count the phrases in the following obituary. Compare your findings with those of other students.

Gregory Peck 1916–2003

Known for his baritone voice and measured delivery, Gregory Peck seemed to be at home playing a man of strength, dignity and compassion. He is best remembered for his moving portrayal of Atticus Finch, the bespectacled southern small-town lawyer defending a black man unjustly accused of rape. In this 1963 black-and-white film of the novel *To Kill a Mockingbird,* which many students study in school, Peck played a single father of two children, Jem and Scout.

Go Grammar!   69

Not only did Peck portray the stoic endurance of a sincere, principled father, he also enacted the creed of nonviolent resistance. In one scene, a racist white woman spits into Atticus' face. He takes out his handkerchief, wipes away the insult, and walks off in silence. Such is the compelling force of moral dignity put to the test, a virtue that Peck portrayed well.

Like many actors, he played both "good guy" and "bad guy" roles. He enjoyed playing the hero as the commanding officer in *Guns of Navarone,* but he also played convincingly the sinister Dr. Mengele in *The Boys From Brazil*. In public life, Peck campaigned for the Democratic Party. Life was not easy for him, however. He married twice and survived personal tragedy in his family. Through it all, he conducted himself with public reticence, dignity, and tolerance. This was a life worth living, an active and considerate life.

Total number of phrases: _____

Taking It Further

Choose a phrase that appeals to you in the obituary above. Make it the basis of a two-paragraph obituary of someone you admire in this century or from earlier times. Write the obituary in your notebook. Then, exchange your writing with a classmate. Discuss in class: Which qualities do we value in people?

In the Real World

Find a detailed obituary in a newspaper, or print a hard copy of an online obituary for a famous person. Write below at least four phrases that tell you something important about the person's character.

_____

_____

_____

Write a sentence explaining why one phrase appeals to you the most.

_____

_____

LESSON 28
SENTENCES
Clauses

> A **clause** is a group of words that contains a subject and a verb. There are two types of clauses: main and subordinate.
>
> 1 A **main clause** usually makes complete sense on its own and expresses the primary idea of the sentence.
>
> **Example**   The campers returned at twilight.
>
> A sentence can include more than one main clause.
>
> **Example**   The national anthem ended and the crowd roared in anticipation of the game to come. (two main clauses)
>
> 2 A **subordinate clause** is less important than the main clause in a sentence. It offers extra information and cannot stand alone. A subordinate clause begins with an introductory word such as if, that, when, or because (see Lesson 16).
>
> **Example**   The campers returned at twilight **because** they had taken a wrong turn.
>   main clause   subordinate clause

Try It Out

Identify whether each sentence consists of one main clause, two main clauses, or one main clause and one subordinate clause.

1 I wanted to watch the special, but it was getting late. _____

2 The dog chased the boys for several minutes. _____

3 If you don't like to cook, you can chop vegetables.

_____

4 I was thinking about my homework when something happened.

_____

5 Bill can't stand heavy metal music. _____

6 My favorite band is playing at the festival. _____

7 The twins will tell us about the tournament after they get home.

_____

8 I'd love to have a dog, but taking on a pet is too much work. _____

9 Matt knew that he'd left his wallet in the car.

_____

10 Unless I finish early, I won't be able to go.

_____

Taking It Further

Underline the main clauses and circle the subordinate clauses in the following real-estate advertisement.

13 Rose Drive
Beautiful and quiet, this wonderful location is a place where your life can flourish. This recently remodeled family home has a beautiful garden, which provides a living representation of the street's name. Besides the graceful living room, a kitchen with the latest appliances gives your family a comfortable gathering space. A laundry and double garage complete this ideal location, and nearby shops and schools make it particularly convenient.

In the Real World

Read the following start to a suspense story. Plan and write the second paragraph to the story. Include two main clauses and a subordinate clause in your paragraph. Underline the two main clauses and circle the subordinate clause.

I saw an alien last night. Its purple, oblong head with telescoping eyes flashed past me like that of a hyper praying mantis, and the creature disappeared into the shadows out of view of my bedroom window. That was not the end of its visit, though.

_____

_____

_____

_____

_____

_____

REVISION TEST 7 Sentences

Review Lessons 24–28 before completing this test.

1 Rewrite these declarative sentences as imperative sentences.

  a You should stay on the right side of the path.

  _____

  b You shouldn't drive in the fog with the headlights on high.

  _____

2 Rewrite these stringy sentences as shorter sentences.

  a We came home exhausted from the camp, yet we were thrilled we had passed all the tests on the obstacle course, and it was great that everyone in our class enjoyed one another's company for the weekend.

  _____

  _____

  _____

  b First we caught the Galveston ferry to spend the afternoon at the beach, but once on board Mando and Angie wanted to go to the Space Center instead, so we had to take the ferry back.

  _____

  _____

  _____

3 Rewrite the following sentences to avoid dangling modifiers.

  Example   Running along the beach, a ship appeared on the horizon.
  While I was running along the beach, a ship appeared on the horizon.

  a Waiting for the bus in the rain, an old schoolmate waved from a passing car.

  _____

  _____

  b Running to score a goal, the referee blew his whistle.

  _____

  _____

NAME _____   DATE _____

4 Read the following passage and complete the exercise below.

> Passion. A driving force. We often hear today the importance of having a passion for what we like to do. Passion can give you that push ahead to achieve difficult challenges. Sitting in the comfort zone, opportunities can pass by. Passion is a strong emotion or drive to do something that we all can feel, but not all people boother to nurture it, and they may start blaming others for their own lack of progress or success, which is not a responsible attitude. Seize the day!

List an example of each of the following.

a Sentence fragments _____

b Imperative sentence _____

c Stringy sentence _____

_____

_____

_____

d Dangling modifier _____

5 Underline each main clause and circle each subordinate clause in the following passage.

> Since the United States was founded on a single Constitution, there must be one way to interpret it, right? Actually, approaches to the Constitution fall into one of two camps. Some people believe that we should read the Constitution as closely as possible to its literal meaning. Others support applying it to situations not specifically mentioned by the Founders.

NAME _____   DATE _____

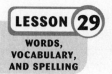

Synonyms and Antonyms

A **synonym** is a word that has a meaning similar to that of another word. Synonyms are the same part of speech but convey different shades of meaning.

Example   exciting (adj.)   Synonyms: thrilling, stimulating, enthralling

An **antonym** is a word that has a meaning opposite to that of another word. Antonyms are the same part of speech as their opposites.

Example   tall (adj.)   Antonyms: short, little, petite

Try It Out

1   First, choose the correct synonym or antonym from the box below, as indicated. Then, add another synonym or antonym of your own.

love	forgive	concern	courage	damage
false	adventurous	kind	suspicious	accept
deceit	inhabit	discover	honesty	shun

Example   hate (antonym) ___love (from the list); adoration (own choice)___

a reject (antonym)   _____

b dishonesty (synonym)   _____

c sympathy (synonym)   _____

d occupy (synonym)   _____

2   Choose four other words from the list above. Write an antonym for each word in a sentence to show its meaning.

Example   ___(love) Romeo and Juliet were victims of <u>hate</u> between their families.___

a _____

b _____

c _____

d _____

Taking It Further

Improve this text by writing two synonyms for each word in bold. Use a dictionary to make sure that your choice of synonyms fits the context of each sentence.

> I cannot wait to **get** a mobile phone for my birthday. All my friends have their own so it's been **hard** not having one. Dad has been **uncertain** for a while, but Mom thinks it's **appropriate** for me to have my own phone.

_____

_____

In the Real World

1   Replace some of the words in this advertisement with synonyms. Circle the words in the advertisement and write your own synonyms beside it.

2   Choose another advertisement from a magazine or newspaper. Rewrite it in your notebook as an amusing "anti-advertisement" by replacing words with their antonyms.

Example   Choose Sopesudz for a filthier, duller wash!

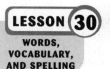

LESSON 30 Using a Thesaurus

WORDS, VOCABULARY, AND SPELLING

A **thesaurus** is a book of words and their related ideas. It is a useful reference text for anyone who wants to write and speak effectively and precisely.

You can find a synonym or antonym for almost any given word or phrase in the thesaurus (see Lesson 29).

To use a thesaurus, follow these steps:

1 Look up the word for which you want synonyms or antonyms, or use the thesaurus feature on your word processor.

2 Choose carefully the word or expression that is most appropriate to your requirements.

3 Use a dictionary to double-check the meaning of the word you have chosen.

Try It Out

1 Below are ten words in random order. Rewrite them in alphabetical order in the chart at the bottom of the page.

renown	apprehend	retrieve	grow	alienate
acquire	mediate	mentor	propose	doubt

2 Beside each word in the table, write three synonyms from your thesaurus.

Example   justify — (1) excuse, (2) defend, (3) rationalize

Word	Synonym 1	Synonym 2	Synonym 3
1.			
2.			
3.			
4.			
5.			
6.			

Word	Synonym 1	Synonym 2	Synonym 3
7.			
8.			
9.			
10.			

Taking It Further

Find in your thesaurus the most appropriate synonym for each italicized word.

Example   The girl spoke *softly* to the class. _____quietly_____

1   The volunteer fire brigade worked *heroically* to contain the fires. _____

2   She seemed very *upset*, so people left her alone. _____

3   During the heat wave, people *rushed* to the beach. _____

4   The game *resumed* once the spectators left the field. _____

In the Real World

Rewrite the following passage by replacing the words in bold with more vivid words chosen from your thesaurus.

When a family is **busy**, eating at home can be hard. Picking up fast food can seem **easy** and **handy**. Fixing dinner can be worth the **work**, though. A home-cooked meal not only **gives** everyone a chance to **work together**, but also is often more nutritious.

_____

_____

_____

_____

LESSON (31) Word Origins

WORDS, VOCABULARY, AND SPELLING

English is a rich, vibrant language that continues to grow and change. Our language has its origins in the Germanic languages spoken in northern Europe. Over time, words have come into English from Latin, Gaelic, Norse, French, Greek, Arabic, and other languages.

There can be three parts to a word: the root word, the prefix, and the suffix (see Lessons 17 and 18). Any or all of these parts might have derived from different languages.

For example, the prefixes *un-* and *mis-* come from Old English; *dis-* and *in-* come from Latin. They are all negative prefixes.

Examples **un**helpful, **dis**harmony, **in**hospitable, **mis**judge

Because these word parts have different origins and slightly different meanings, it may be difficult to use them correctly. Notice the difference between **un**treated and **mis**treated, **dis**able and **un**able, **un**organized and **dis**organized.

A good dictionary will give you the origins of words. However, a concise students' dictionary may not provide such detail.

Example

> **magazine • n.** a periodical publication containing articles and illustrations; a regular television or radio program comprising a variety of items. **2.** a chamber for holding a supply of cartridges to be fed automatically into the breech of a gun. **3.** a store for arms, ammunitions, and explosives
>
> — ORIGIN 16th c.: from Fr. *magasin*, from Ital. *magazzino*, from Arab. *makzin, makzan* "storehouse"
>
> *Concise Oxford English Dictionary*, 10th ed. Oxford: Oxford University Press, 1999.

This definition gives us the various meanings of *magazine*. It also tells us that it is a noun that entered English in the sixteenth century from the French word *magasin*, which was based on an Italian word which, in turn, was derived from an Arabic word. Although the original term was an Arabic one, it came into English via two other languages: Italian and French. What a complex history for such a common word!

Try It Out

1 Look up each word in your dictionary and write its meaning.

a untreated _____

b mistreated _____

c unable _____

d disable _____

2 Now use each word correctly in a separate sentence.

a untreated _____

_____

b mistreated _____

_____

c unable _____

_____

d disable _____

_____

Taking It Further

For each root word, list some English words that are derived from the same origin.

Root word	Meaning	English words
capo (L)	head, captain	
centum (L)	hundred	
mono (Gk)	one	
terra (L)	earth	
logos (Gk)	word, study	
drifan (OE)	to go with wind or tide	
bitan (OE)	to bite	

In the Real World

1 Using information from your dictionary, write the origins of the words listed below. If your dictionary gives such information, include the date each word first appeared in written English.

Word	Language of Origin	Date of First Recorded Use
frolic	Dutch < Middle Dutch	16th century
icicle		
moccasin		
curfew	ME <	
festival	ME < MF <	
tomato		
couch		
mortuary		
kangaroo		
tongue		
genre		
coffee		
tattoo		
boycott		
guru		
street		
monotonous		
circus		
dinghy		

2 Design a timeline showing when the words in the table above entered English. Indicate the language(s) of origin. Use the space below for your draft.

3 Present the timeline to the class in any form you consider appropriate, such as a poster, PowerPoint presentation, or lecture.

LESSON 32 **Spelling for Good Writing**

WORDS, VOCABULARY, AND SPELLING

You can improve your spelling through regular practice.
Here is a method for practicing your spelling, using the word *accountable* as an example.

1   Copy the word and say it aloud to yourself. Then, split the word into sound units: ac/count/able.

2   Write a brief memory prompt by focusing on a letter or letters that cause any confusion. For example, the first part is *a* and *c*. The second part of the word is *count*, with an *ou*, just like the word *count*. The third part ends in *-able*, **not** *-ible*. Your memory prompt can be *A C   Count   Able*.

3   Each night learn a small number of spelling words this way, say four or more. Then, ask a member of your family or another student to test you.

Remember that you must identify a way to learn a word to help your brain remember the correct spelling.

Commonly Mispelled Words

aisle	efficiency	legislature	reference
amateur	explain		rehearsal
ancient	explanatory	miscellaneous	reign
		mortgage	remedy
balloon	fragile	mosquito	reservoir
beauty	frequent	movement	
beautiful	frequency	movable	seize
beautifully			society
beginning	gauge	nuclear	
brief	guess	numb	terrific
bureau			tonight
bureaucratic	heir	obey	
	hypothesis	opaque	vacuum
capacity	hypothetical	ought	villain
certain		outrageous	virtue
conscience	initial		virus
conscious	initiative	particle	
cough		physician	wreath
courtesy	jeopardy	psychological	
courteous	justice	protein	yolk
	justifiable		
damage		quantity	
deceive	knowledgeable	quarrel	
		quotient	

Go Grammar!

Some Confusing Words

Some words might sound similar but have different meanings and uses. It helps to know the part of speech of the word, as well as its dictionary meaning. Read the list below and check at least four pairs that you find confusing or did not know. Then, write a sentence for each word showing its proper use.

allusion (n. indirect reference)
illusion (n. false impression)

awe (n. fearful wonder)
aw (interj. of disappointment or pity)

credulous (adj. gullible)
credible (adj. believable)

elicit (v. obtain information)
illicit (adj. illegal)

explicit (adj. clearly stated)
implicit (adj. suggsted)

imply (v. suggest)
infer (v. guess)

secede (v. to withdraw from a nation)
succeed (v. to accomplish a goal)

tortuous (adj. winding)
torturous (adj. extremely painful)

_____

_____

_____

_____

_____

_____

_____

_____

_____

_____

_____

_____

Tricky Spelling Words

Here are some important rules that can help improve your spelling.

1 When the sound is "ee," put *i* before *e* except after *c*.

Examples thieve, achieve, grieve, receive, deceive, perceive

Note: Some words do not follow this rule — *either, neither, seize, weird.*

2 To form the plural of a word ending in *y*, change the *y* to *i* and add *es.*

Examples library, libraries; diary, diaries; lady, ladies; story, stories

3 The rule above applies to words that have a consonant before the *y*. If there is a vowel before the *y*, form the plural by adding *s*.

Examples key, keys; monkey, monkeys; journey, journeys

Try It Out

1 Check the spelling of the following words. Rewrite those that are incorrect, and place a checkmark by those that are already correct.

beleif _____   deceive _____

reciept _____   wierd _____

mischief _____   freind _____

2 Make the following words plural.

lobby _____   donkey _____

baby _____   weekday _____

trolley _____   cherry _____

Taking It Further

Write a sentence for each of these easily confused words to show the correct meaning. Use a dictionary if you need to.

Example   allude/elude __You allude to Shakespeare when you say,__ __"Parting is such sweet sorrow." Some students try to__ __elude a late penalty by claiming computer problems.__

1 avenge/revenge _____

_____

2 diary/dairy _____

_____

3 key/quay _____

_____

4 notorious/famous _____

_____

5 persecute/prosecute _____

_____

6 restive/restful _____

_____

In the Real World

It's time to have a bit of fun. Write an advertisement with at least two deliberate misspellings. Then, exchange your work with that of another student, and try to find the mistakes in each other's work.

_____

_____

_____

REVISION TEST 8 Words, Vocabulary, and Spelling

Review Lessons 29–33 before completing this test.

1 Write two synonyms for each of the following words.

a delight (n.) _____

b sadness (n.) _____

c anger (n.) _____

d give (v.) _____

2 Write two antonyms for each of the following words.

a quiet (adj.) _____

b ugly (adj.) _____

c interesting (adj.) _____

d polite (adj.) _____

3 Form antonyms for each of the following words by writing the prefix mis-, il-, mal-, or im-.

a _____ moderate   **d** _____ nourish   **g** _____ manage

b _____ spell   **e** _____ literate   **h** _____ logical

c _____ mortal   **f** _____ possible

4 Circle the incorrect spellings in the following passage. Then, spell the words correctly on the lines below the passage.

Storys for young readers used to be known for the rosie picture they painted of the world. Recent works, however, present more complicatted situations. Several popular titles place their young heros in dark surroundings. Their sucess comes from having to make decisions in difficult circumstances, to percieve good or decieve a bully, to avenge something hurtful or devize a creative solution — all this makes for colorful tales that are eagerly sought in librarys and bookstores.

_____

_____

5 Circle the incorrect spellings in the following review of a popular film. Then, spell the words correctly on the lines below the passage.

This beautifull and moveing film explores the universeal themes of love, rejection, and the surch for identity in the world. The caracters are acountable for their decisions, and a tribal girl finds her destany. The movie captures your sole as it mixes education and entertainment, oferring something special for everyone.

_____

_____

6 Write a sentence for each of these easily confused words to show its correct meaning.

a key/quay _____

_____

b angel/angle _____

_____

c implied/inferred _____

_____

d allusion/illusion _____

_____

Go Grammar!

LESSON 34 Formal Letters
WRITING IN CONTEXT

There are several situations that require you to write a formal letter: applying for a job, writing a letter to the editor of a newspaper, giving or seeking information, or making a complaint. Read the following letters, and note the structure and the tone of each.

Example 1

Give your full address, including e-mail if you have it, and your phone number.

Katherine Burdon
53 Simpson Street
Brentwood, TN 37027
Tel: (615) 555-7614
E-mail: KBurdon@bigpond.net

Include the date after your address.

May 5, 2006

Include full details of addressee.

Mr. John Stecka, Manager
Music City Supply
132 Brooks Highway
Nashville, TN 37202

Use a formal mode of address.

Dear Mr. Stecka:

Clearly state your purpose.

I am writing to apply for the position of Sales Assistant, advertised in the *Nashville Post* on May 3.

Introduce yourself.

I am fifteen years old, and I believe that I have the experience and the personal qualities your company is looking for.

Add supporting material.

I have had a paper route for the last two years, and during this time I have been reliable, honest, and trustworthy. As freshman class president at Roby High School, I set up a social service program in which students read to local elderly people.

Mention enclosures and invite further contact.

Enclosed please find my résumé. I look forward to discussing the position with you in person.

Use an appropriate closing and include a printed version of your name, as well as your signature.

Yours sincerely,

Katherine Burdon

Katherine Burdon

Example 2

James Johnson
32 Banks Street
Ocean City, MD 21843

July 25, 2006

Council Member Patty Marks
City Hall
301 N. Baltimore Avenue
Ocean City, MD 21842

Dear Ms. Marks:

I am writing to complain about the construction currently taking place on my street. Since work began, daytime noise levels have been unbearable.

I ask for the Council's help in improving this uncomfortable situation.

Sincerely,

James Johnson

James Johnson

Example 3

Peter Radcliffe
9314 Cook Drive
Carson City, NV 89701

October 15, 2006

Archivist
Carson High School
1111 N. Saliman
Carson City, NV 89701

Dear Sir or Madam:

I graduated from Carson High School in 1967 and am organizing my class's forty-year reunion. I would be grateful for copies of any photos you may have of our senior prom. I will pay any copying costs incurred.

Many thanks,

Peter Radcliffe

Peter Radcliffe

Recently, e-mails have replaced letters in many situations (refer to Lesson 40). Remember that if your purpose is formal, then your structure and tone should also be formal, even in an e-mail message.

Try It Out

Look again at each of the letters above. Identify the purpose of each letter, and list the main points each writer makes.

Example 1

Purpose: _____

Main points: _____

Example 2

Purpose: _____

Main points: _____

Example 3

Purpose: _____

Main points: _____

Taking It Further

1   What problems can you see with the following letters?

Dear Mr. Jones:

I'd like a job at your shop. I have to pass it every day on the way to and from school, so I would be there every day anyway. I like computer games and so I know a fair bit about them. Working in a shop that sold them would be cool. I'll call in on Thursday to get your answer.

Jake Flanagan

_____

_____

_____

Mr. Whitworth:

I live on the same street, and I am telling you not to let you dog out of your yard. It has dug up my flower beds and terrorized my cat. How would you like it if I did that to you?

—A Neighbor

_____

_____

_____

2 Rewrite the letters above, showing how you would have written them.

_____

_____

_____

_____

_____

_____

_____

_____

In the Real World

In your notebook, write the following letters, including addresses and all other necessary details.

- To the manager of a dry-cleaning firm, complaining about a damaged article of clothing
- To the local bus system, asking about something you left on the bus
- To a local business, applying for a summer job.

Informal Letters

LESSON 35
WRITING IN CONTEXT

There are many types of informal writing: personal letters and e-mails, journals, notes, postcards, and so forth. A strong personal voice is most important in this style of communication.

We write to people we know for a variety of purposes:

- to give or receive information
- to thank someone
- to convey emotions and keep in touch.

Example 1

Dear Jan, ◄─────────────────────────── Identify addressee

Thanks for the information about next month's meeting ◄─── Opening statement — establish connection with addressee
of the Nature Guild.

Should I bring my laptop to the meeting to take notes? ◄─── Indicate purpose: seeking information

Cheers, ◄─────────────────────────── Appropriate closing
Paula ◄─────────────────────────── Identify sender

Example 2

Dear Kara,
Having a great time. Weather
fantastic, surf terrific!
It'll be tough to head home.

See you soon.
Luv,
Helen

xoxoxoxoxoxo

Kara Smith
24 Corrinna Rd
Boise, ID 83704

Example 3

Dear Aunt Genevieve,

Thank you so much for the great present you sent last week. I know you never forget my birthday, and I always look forward to seeing what you've sent. The subscription to Skateboard Universe is terrific.

My skateboarding skills were improving right up to the time I broke my leg and my wrist. That's what I get for not wearing my gear!

I'm really looking forward to getting back on the board, but I'll be able to read the magazine while I'm recuperating.

Lots of love,
Joseph

P.S. I should be out of my casts by the end of the month.

Try It Out

Make a bulleted list of what you would include in the following letters.

Example   To the secretary of your rock-climbing club, asking for information

- _____
- _____
- _____

1   To a friend's mother in whose home you stayed for a week

- _____
- _____
- _____

2   To your swimming coach, explaining your absence from a recent swim meet

- _____
- _____
- _____

3 To a relative who is in the hospital

- _____
- _____
- _____

Taking It Further

1 From one of the bulleted lists above, draft an appropriate letter in full (including addresses and appropriate opening and closing phrases). Write the letter in your notebook.

2 Use the other two plans as the basis for composing a postcard and a personal diary entry. Write them in your notebook.

In the Real World

Read the following passage. It is a short story told in letter form. In a separate notebook, write your own short story using this style.

Wednesday, 4 June
Dear Mr. Morgan,
You will be surprised to have a letter from me since we are living in the same house but I should like to remind you that you have not paid me board for the last week.

Yours sincerely,
Mabel Doris Morgan
(landlady)

Wednesday, 11 June
Dear Mr. Morgan,
This is to remind you that you are now owing two weeks' board and I should like to take the opportunity to ask you to remove the outboard motor from your room. There is an oil stain on the rug already and I'm afraid for my curtains and bedspread.

Yours sincerely,
Mabel Doris Morgan
(landlady)

Friday, 20 June

Dear Mr. Morgan,

No. Black oil and grease will not wash out of a sheet. . . . I am afraid I shall have to ask you to move the outboard motor again as it is impossible for anyone to sit in the lounge room to watch TV the way you have the propeller balanced between two easy chairs.

> Yours sincerely,
> Mabel D. Morgan
> (landlady)

Wednesday, 25 June

Dear Mr. Morgan,

Thank you for the two dollars. I should like to remind you that you now owe four weeks' board less two dollars.

> Yours sincerely,
> Mabel D. Morgan
> (landlady)

Wednesday, 2 July

Dear Mr. Morgan,

Board is up to five weeks. With respect, Mr. Morgan, I'd like to suggest you try to get a job. I'd like to suggest the way to do this is to get up early and get the paper. . . . I'd like to say this has to be done early and quick. Mr. Morgan, five weeks' board is five weeks' board. And Mr. Morgan, what's been going on in the bathroom? I think I am entitled to an explanation.

> Yours sincerely,
> Mabel Doris Morgan
> (landlady)

Friday, 11 July

Mr. Morgan,

Get a job. And clean your room. I never saw such a mess of chocolate papers under anyone's bed, ever. In my whole life I never saw such a mess. . . . I'd like to remind you how to get a job. You get up early to get a job. . . .

> Yours sincerely,
> Mabel Doris Morgan
> (landlady)

And Mr. Morgan, Bathroom? Explanation? And Mr. Morgan. Smoking!

> "Wednesdays and Fridays" by Elizabeth Jolley, in *Personal Best*,
> G. Disher, ed. Sydney: Angus and Robertson, 1989.

NAME _____   DATE _____

**LESSON 36**
WRITING IN CONTEXT

Basic Paragraphs

Paragraphs are the essential building blocks of essays and narratives.

A paragraph begins with a **topic sentence** that identifies the main idea or focus.

A paragraph is developed through several **sentences** that explain or illustrate the main idea outlined in the topic sentence. These sentences must be relevant and logically organized. A paragraph finishes with a **concluding sentence** that summarizes the main idea.

The first line of a paragraph is indented. Alternatively, in some kinds of writing a blank line may be placed between paragraphs. Generally, paragraphs vary in length: 25 to 250 words or 1 to 10 sentences are basic guidelines for length.

Example

Topic sentence
Indent

Explanatory
sentences

Concluding
sentence

> Gary Soto is one of America's most successful poets and writers for young people. Soto was born in Fresno, California, in 1952. Soto's fiction draws on his experience of growing up in a poor Mexican-American family. He made up for the lack of reading at home by studying and pursuing writing on his own. He has received numerous honors for such collections as *Living up the Street* and his film *The Pool Party*. Regardless of genre, Soto has consistently entertained and challenged his readers.

Try It Out

Read the three-paragraph article below and complete the tasks as indicated.

1   The paragraphs have been run together. Place double strokes (//) to indicate the paragraph breaks. (There are two.)

The Deadly Brown Snake

Another deadly Australian species is the brown snake. Its poison is reckoned to be the second most powerful in the world. One evening in December 1991, some friends were sitting on the banks of the Murray River when they saw a swimming snake. Rashly, one of them jumped in, swam after it and seized hold of it. As he took it back to the bank, it bit him on the hand. Returning to the bank, the angry swimmer killed the snake. His worried friends called for an ambulance, and he was taken to [a] hospital, but his heart stopped and he died on the way. The snake turned out to be a brown snake. The man died just over half an hour after being bitten. About 3000 Australians are bitten by poisonous snakes every year — but thanks to the development and availability of anti-venom, deaths from snakebite are the exception today. Between 1981 and 1991, only 18 deaths from snakebite were reported to the Melbourne Laboratories.

True Horror Stories by Terrance Dicks. New York: Sterling, 1997. p. 89.

2 Rewrite the topic sentence as a question. _____

_____

3 Write a concluding sentence for the final paragraph. _____

_____

Taking It Further

Match the notes in the following box with the appropriate topic sentence below, and write the notes after the topic sentence. Then, organize the notes into a logical order and write each paragraph in your notebook.

• Includes island of Tasmania   • Extensive deserts
• Convicts used as labor to establish Australian colony   • Nomadic hunter-gatherers in small family clans
• Covers a land area of 7,682,300 square km   • Prison ships on England's River Thames dangerously overcrowded
• Britain had extensive convict problem due to economic and social changes resulting in widespread poverty   • Complex spiritual beliefs based on "The Dreamtime," when mythic beings created the world
• Population of 17,843,000 live along coastal areas   • Newly independent American colonies refused to accept convicts
• Arrived 40,000 to 60,000 years ago from Asia   • Great Dividing Range and Barrier Reef are significant geographical features

Topic sentences

1 Anthropologists believe that indigenous Australians arrived during the last Ice Age.

_____

_____

_____

2 Why did the British government decide to send convicts to Australia?

_____

_____

_____

_____

3 Australia is a significant continent and country in the Asia-Pacific region.

_____

_____

_____

_____

In the Real World

1 Journalists are trained to write concise introductory paragraphs for their news articles. Introductory paragraphs must answer these questions: *Who? What? Where?* and *When?*

Read the following news extract and complete the comprehension chart that follows.

A Qantas 737-800 carrying 126 passengers flew on one engine and made an unscheduled landing in Cairns after a flying fox was sucked into the engine. The drama began about 7 p.m. on Sunday night over Cairns airport, just as Flight 800 bound for Darwin lifted off.

The Age. August 19, 2003. p. 6.

Who? _____

What? _____

Where? _____

When? _____

2 Find an article from a newspaper. Cut out the opening paragraph of the article, paste it in the space below, and complete the comprehension chart that follows.

Title _____

Author _____

Newspaper _____

Date _____

Who? _____

What? _____

Where? _____

When? _____

3 Write your own paragraph-long article on a news event in your school or neighborhood. Be sure to include information covering the four basic questions: *Who? What? Where?* and *When?*

_____

_____

_____

_____

_____

NAME _____   DATE _____

Informative Paragraphs

> **Informative paragraphs** explain and illustrate information on a particular topic such as a person, place, event, or process. Such paragraphs include relevant definitions, facts, and examples relating to the topic. Informative paragraphs are used in reports, biographies, non-fiction writing, and reference works. See Lesson 36 for more on paragraph structure.

Try It Out

Read the informative paragraph below about vampires. Underline a definition, circle an example, and identify a fact with a wavy underline.

> Vampire, in folklore, is a corpse that rises from the grave during the night, often in the form of a bat, and for nourishment sucks the blood of sleeping humans. Various talismans and herbs supposedly avert vampires, but, according to tradition, they can be destroyed only by cremation or by stakes driven through their hearts. Belief in vampires originated in ancient times and was especially widespread among the Slavs. The novel *Dracula* (1897) by the British writer Bram Stoker tells the story of the Transylvanian vampire Count Dracula, who became one of the most popular subjects of horror films.

> *Microsoft Encarta Encyclopedia 97*, World English Edition.

Taking It Further

The following sentences inform about the cause and effects of acid rain. However, the sentences are out of order. Write them in the correct order in paragraph form.

- Eventually, the acid pollutants fall to earth through rain, snow, or fog.
- Acid rain is a form of air pollution that causes serious environmental damage.
- These pollutants may be transported long distances from their source by wind conditions or in clouds.
- Acid rain has poisoned lakes and forests, eroded structures and caused acid smog in cities, and mutated plants and animals.
- Acid rain occurs when industrial emissions like sulphur and nitrogen combine with atmospheric moisture.

_____

_____

_____

_____

_____

_____

_____

In the Real World

Use the following facts to write an informative paragraph about sharks. Your paragraph must include a topic sentence, explanatory sentences in logical order, and a concluding sentence. Carefully consider the organization of the facts.

Facts about sharks: grey, leathery skin; 368 species; 5 to 7 gills behind head; rigid dorsal fin and tail; rows of teeth; types — whale shark (biggest = 15 meters), great white shark (most well known), hammerhead shark (most aggressive); fast-swimming; live in tropical or sub-tropical waters; scavenge and hunt for food.

_____

_____

_____

_____

_____

_____

_____

_____

_____

_____

_____

Writing an Essay

LESSON 38
WRITING IN CONTEXT

The basic **essay** structure includes five paragraphs — one introductory paragraph, three body paragraphs, and a conclusion. However, additional body paragraphs may be included, depending on the topic and detail required.

The **introductory paragraph** identifies the subject of the essay. It defines key terms and gives a brief outline of the points that will be raised in the essay.

Body paragraphs expand on the subject. Each paragraph has a specific focus and incorporates a topic sentence, explanatory sentences, and a concluding sentence. Body paragraphs provide examples, facts and figures, definitions, key vocabulary, explanations, and causes/effects.

The **concluding paragraph** summarizes the key ideas stated about the subject.

In general, a five-paragraph essay is 600 to 800 words in length.

Try It Out

Read the introductory paragraph and first body paragraph of the essay below. Answer the questions that follow.

Essay Topic   **Explain the dominant style of architecture from three different historical periods**

As people change, so do the buildings in which they live and work. The history of architecture, the art of building, offers a fascinating look at how people have shaped their environment and expressed their cultures. Three styles of architecture stand out in the history of Western Europe: Romanesque, Gothic, and _____ (STYLE OF YOUR CHOICE).

Romanesque architecture developed from the building style of ancient Rome. Although the Roman Empire no longer existed by 500 A.D., Europeans highly valued its culture. For centuries they tried to reproduce Roman literature, law, and, yes, buildings. By the year 1000, Roman architecture had developed into a simpler and more solid form. This style came to be called Romanesque because it was "Roman-like." Romanesque buildings have thick walls, rounded arches and vaulted ceilings, and heavy support structures.

1 Write out the definition of a key term used in the introductory paragraph.

_____

2 Write out the topic sentence from the first body paragraph.

_____

3 Give one example of a historical fact from the first body paragraph.

_____

_____

4 Give an example of a key term from the first body paragraph and its definition.

_____

_____

5 Write a concluding sentence for the first body paragraph.

_____

Taking It Further

The essay above is incomplete. Finish it by completing the following tasks.

1 According to the introduction, the second body paragraph is about Gothic architecture. Write the second body paragraph on the lines provided, using the following information.

Gothic architecture developed in the 12th century.	Gothic buildings can therefore be much taller and let in more light than Romanesque ones.	Pointed arches and intricate decorations are typical of Gothic buildings.
Distributing the weight of the building to piers and buttresses made for thinner walls.	The term "Gothic" was applied later by artists who thought this style was crude and barbarian, like the ancient Goths.	This style dominated the Middle Ages, lasting until the 16th century.

NAME _____ DATE _____

Second Body Paragraph

Topic sentence: _____

_____

Explanatory sentence 1: _____

_____

Explanatory sentence 2: _____

_____

Explanatory sentence 3: _____

_____

Explanatory sentence 4: _____

_____

Concluding sentence: _____

_____

2 Choose a later period of architecture such as the Renaissance or Neoclassical style. First, conduct some basic research on the style and write your notes into the chart below. Then, complete the paragraph on the lines provided.

Architectural Style: _____

- _____   - _____
- _____   - _____
- _____   - _____
- _____   - _____

Third Body Paragraph

Topic sentence: _____

_____

Explanatory sentence 1: _____

_____

Explanatory sentence 2: _____

_____

Go Grammar! (105)

Explanatory sentence 3: _____

_____

Explanatory sentence 4: _____

_____

Concluding sentence: _____

_____

3 Write a conclusion for the essay.

_____

_____

_____

_____

_____

In the Real World

Students are often required to write essays outlining the changes and developments experienced by characters in stories or novels.

Select a character from a story or novel that you are currently studying, and complete the following essay outline by inserting appropriate responses. This essay outline is a model only — you may alter words or phrases in the sentences to reflect your own style.

Essay Topic   Outline the changes in the central character of a story or novel.

1   Introductory Paragraph
Write one sentence outlining the essay topic.
Write one sentence summarizing the text you are writing about.
Write one sentence briefly outlining the development of the central character.

Example   In novels characters experience major changes and developments. *Great Expectations* by Charles Dickens is set in nineteenth-century England and explores the changes in the main character, Pip. In the novel, Pip changes from an innocent boy to a selfish snob and finally to an honest and likeable young man.

_____

_____

_____

2 First Body Paragraph

At the beginning of the story/novel, _____ (main character's name)

is _____ and _____ (two adjectives

to describe the character's personality). As _____ (main character's

name) is described early in the story: _____

_____

_____

_____

(insert a quote from the text — use quotation marks, give page number). This suggests

that _____

_____

(comment on what the quote reveals about the main character).

3 Second Body Paragraph

Things start to change for _____ (main character's name) when

_____

(incident where the main character starts to change). This shows that _____

_____

(comment on what the turning point reveals about the main character). An additional

turning point is _____

_____

(another incident where the main character changes). This demonstrates that _____

_____

(comment on what the turning point reveals about the main character).

4 Third Body Paragraph

By the end of the story/novel, _____ (insert main character's name)

has become _____ and _____ (adjectives

describing the main character). The following quote illustrates this transformation:

_____

(insert a quote from the text — use quotation marks, give page number). _____

_____

(comment on what the quote reveals about the main character).

5 Conclusion

The growth of _____ (insert main character's name) as a character

shapes the entire story/novel. _____

_____

_____

(explain how understanding these changes helps the reader understand the story/novel as

a whole).

LESSON 39
WRITING IN CONTEXT

Emotional Language

Emotional language is designed to appeal to the reader's feelings. There are many examples in today's print media and advertising of emotional language, such as big, bold headlines in newspapers.

Examples Tragic Loss to England in Match

Look at a variety of popular magazines and newspapers to see similar examples of emotionally charged language.

You should be cautious about writing in an emotional style. Meaning and accuracy can be lost if you merely exaggerate the subject of your writing.

Be aware of these three types of emotional expression:

Hyperbole (pronounced "high-PER-bo-lee") is an exaggeration not meant to be taken literally.

Example   I must have waited for **a thousand years.**

A **cliché** is an overused phrase or comment that has lost its meaning.

Example   Don't worry; **every cloud has a silver lining.**

A **superlative** is an adverb or adjective that expresses the highest quality or degree. Superlatives can be overused when praising someone.

Example   These graduates are our **best** and **brightest** ever.

Try It Out

1 State whether each sentence contains *hyperbole*, a *cliché*, or a *superlative*.

Example   When the going gets tough, the tough get going. _*cliché*_

a If I don't get the latest video game, I'll simply die. _____

b He's the greatest thinker since Albert Einstein. _____

c Life is not meant to be easy. _____

d Kathy is the most beautiful girl in the school. _____

e If we don't win, we might as well all stop playing and take up knitting. _____

2 Write two clichés for each of the following situations.

Example   failure _1. It was meant to be. 2. You win some, you lose some._

a Luck _____

_____

b The value of family life _____

_____

c Saving money _____

_____

Taking It Further

1 Rewrite this emotional news report. Replace the emotional words in bold with more appropriate neutral words.

Junk Food Addiction
Junk food could be as **diabolically** addictive as cigarettes or heroin, according to **explosive** research that could pave the way for **massive** lawsuits against manufacturers. The **shocking** findings suggest that snacks high in fat or sugar can cause **horrible** changes in the brain similar to those seen in people hooked on smoking or drugs. It could open the **floodgates** for multimillion-dollar actions against **evil** firms by **desperate** customers who say their health has been ruined by an addiction to junk food.

_____

_____

_____

_____

_____

_____

_____

2 Letters of protest and complaint from citizens often appear in newspapers. Find four examples of emotional expression in the following letter to the editor. Then, rewrite each expression in a more neutral style.

Emotional Expression	Neutral Style
Example glaringly obvious	**Example** clear

Dear Editor,

I completely disagree with your idiotic point of view in yesterday's editorial.

How can you say that schools should not extend their class time to 5 p.m. weekdays?

It's glaringly obvious that the school day is far too short from 9 a.m. to 3:30 p.m.! Kids are spoiled rotten by playing lots of sports, learning instruments, and doing other activities when so much must be crammed into their precious heads before they have to join the workforce.

The other big reason you are wrong is that long-suffering parents should not have to be enslaved with child care arrangements from 3:30 p.m. to dinner time, five days a week. With children staying at school longer each day, parents can stay at work without interruption, safe in the knowledge that our children are imprisoned at school with their heads in books.

Arlene Anderson
Newton, Mass.

3 As the editor, write a thoughtful reply to Ms. Anderson without using emotional language. Make sure you respond to each point Ms. Anderson makes.

_____

_____

_____

_____

_____

_____

In the Real World

Write two emotional media stories for any two of the headlines below. Use hyperbole, clichés, and superlatives to grab the reader's interest with emotional language.

You may wish to study an emotional newspaper report beforehand to imitate the style and layout.

MOVIE STAR'S MARITAL BLUES

BOY, 8, RESCUED FROM HOUSE INFERNO

BANK ROBBERY HERO

EVERYONE'S GOT TO HAVE ONE!

a Headline: _____

Story: _____

_____

_____

_____

_____

b Headline: _____

Story: _____

_____

_____

_____

_____

_____

NAME _____ DATE _____

New Literacies: E-mail and Text Messages

Recent developments in information technology, like e-mail and mobile phones, have helped people to develop a new language — e-language.

E-language is informal and generally does not adhere to traditional grammatical rules. Abbreviations and emoticons are forms of e-language used in e-mail messages and text messages. Many abbreviations are formed from the initial letters of phrases or use numbers to represent words.

Some common acronyms used in e-mails and text messages are:

WU? — What's Up?   FAQ — Frequently Asked Questions

HAND — Have A Nice Day   G2G — Got (to) Go

Emoticons are pictures made from punctuation marks that depict facial expressions (usually when rotated 90 degrees clockwise). Emoticons are used in personal e-mails to express a range of emotions. The word is a combination of *emotion* and *icon*.

Some common emoticons include:

:-D or : -)) for really happy

: 0 for bored

:(or :-(for sad

E-mail and text messages can be easily abused as forms of communication; they may appear irritating or offensive to the recipient. **Netiquette** is the code of conduct concerning e-language. Two main rules concern "shouting" and "flaming."

Typing entirely in capital letters is the electronic equivalent of shouting and should be avoided in e-mails and text messages. When only capital letters are used, they communicate anger. However, capital letters are appropriate for abbreviations (see above).

Standards of punctuation, capitalization, and spelling differ according to whether the e-mail is formal or informal. Completely ignoring standard conventions, however, can confuse the reader.

"Flaming" is the e-mail or text message equivalent to losing your temper or to being aggressive or rude. Never write or send an ill-considered e-mail or text message written in anger. The consequences of doing so can be embarrassing and upsetting for both you and the recipient.

Try It Out

1   The complete expressions below are usually shortened as abbreviations. Write the
    abbreviation for each expression next to it. You may need to use numerals for some words
    (such as 8 for the sound "ate").

Complete expression	Acronym
Thank You Very Much	
In My Humble Opinion	
By The Way	
Bye For Now	
In Other Words	
Laughing to Myself	
For Your Information	
Thanks In Advance	
Evil Grin	
See You Later	

2   Draw each emoticon under the appropriate category in the chart below.

:-/	;->	:-X	:~)	:|	:-*
((( )))***	^^	:"-)	>:-#	:-@	

Happy		Thumbs Up		Hugs and Kisses	
Angry		My Lips Are Sealed		Screaming	
Wink		Kiss		Really down	
Surprised		Confused		So Happy I'm Crying	

3 In groups, brainstorm more abbreviations and emoticons you are familiar with. List them below along with their meanings.

Abbreviation/Emoticon	Meaning
1	
2	
3	
4	
5	
6	
7	
8	
9	
10	

Taking It Further

The following e-mail and text messages do not observe the rules of Netiquette explained above. Read each e-mail message and explain why it is inappropriate.

a hi mom can you please pick me up after school and drive me to the mall because i have to get some stuff for a project also could you advance me some pocket money because I would like to go out for lunch with jack amy sean carrie and mia on saturday thanks mel

_____

b I WOULD HAVE THOUGHT YOU WOULD SUPPORT ME BUT YOU LEFT ME TO FACE THE PRINCIPAL BY MYSELF. NOW I KNOW EXACTLY WHAT TYPE OF FRIEND YOU ARE AND YOU ARE NO FRIEND OF MINE. GET LOST!

_____

In the Real World

1 Draft an e-mail message to a friend in the space below, using a combination of abbreviations and emoticons. Ensure that your message is clear and observes Netiquette. If possible, send the e-mail and attach the reply to this page.

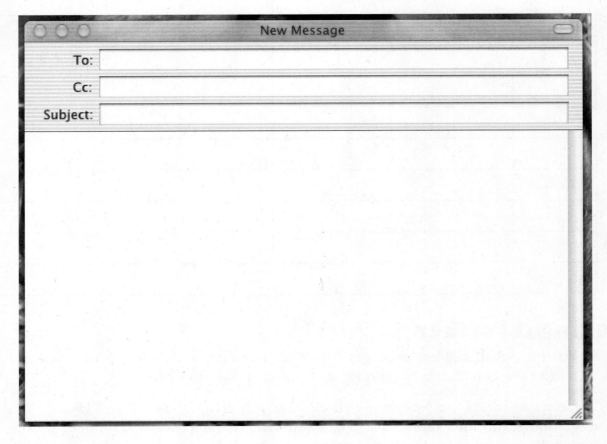

2 Find out one more Netiquette rule. Search the Web by typing in *Netiquette* and check out sites outlining the rules. Write out the rule in the space below and give an example.

_____

_____

_____

3 Share your Netiquette rule with a partner. Write out your partner's Netiquette below.

_____

_____

_____

Acknowledgments

The authors and publisher gratefully credit or acknowledge the following sources for permission to reproduce the following:

Text: *Australian NetGuide,* for extract "Jak 2" in *Australian NetGuide,* Issue 65 (Oct. 2003); Raimondo Cortese, for extract from *The Preacher in the Tower;* David Higham Associates on behalf of Roald Dahl, for extract from *Someone Like You* (Melbourne: Penguin Australia, 1970); Ted Ottley, for extract from "Birthday Boy"; A.P. Watt, Ltd., on behalf of John Branfield, for extracts from *Nancekuke* (Gryphon Books: London, 1988); Oxford University Press, for extract from *Concise Oxford English Dictionary,* 10th ed. (Oxford: Oxford University Press, 1999); Penguin Books Australia, Ltd., for extract "Wednesdays and Fridays" by Elizabeth Jolley, in *Personal Best* (Sydney: Angus and Robertson, 1989); Penguin Books, Ltd., for extract from Lucy Moore, *Con Men and Cutpurses* (Harmondsworth: Penguin, 2000); Robinson Publishing, Ltd., for extract from Terrance Dicks, *True Horror Stories* (London: Robinson Publishing, 1997).

Photographs: The Advertising Archive, Ltd., p. 76.

Every attempt has been made to trace and acknowledge copyright holders. Where the attempt has been unsuccessful, the publisher welcomes information that would redress the situation.

Go Grammar!